EASY SIDE
DISHES
COOKBOOK

The Greatest Low Sodium Side Dish Recipes Ever

(The Yummy Kosher Side Dish Cookbook for All Things Sweet)

Fermin Penton

Published by Alex Howard

Easy Side Dishes Cookbook: The Greatest Low Sodium Side Dish Recipes Ever (The Yummy Kosher Side Dish Cookbook for All Things Sweet)

ISBN 978-1-990169-65-6

Legal & Disclaimer

The information contained in this book is not designed to replace or take the place of any form of medicine or professional medical advice. The information in this book has been provided for educational and entertainment purposes only.

Table of contents

Part 1...1

Introduction 2

Conch Ceviche With Pineapple..........................3

American Ceviche 5

Ecuador Ceviche...7

Crawfish, Crab And Shrimp Ceviche.................9

Moroccan Spiced Sea Bass Ceviche 11

Shrimp Ceviche With Coconut Milk 13

Tomato Shrimp Ceviche....................................15

Basic Ceviche...17

Clamato Shrimp Ceviche...................................19

Simple Ceviche 20

Shiitake Mushroom Ceviche 21

Easy Cauliflower Ceviche..................................23

Raw Vegetable Ceviche 25

Carrot Ceviche..27

Vegan Ceviche...29

Quick Mushroom Ceviche 30

Ceviche With Jalapenos And Red Onions 32

Mexican Mango And White Fish Ceviche..........34

Easy Shrimp Ceviche..36

Swordfish, Squid And Halibut Ceviche 38

Vegan Ceviche Ii... 40

Shrimp Ceviche With Ketchup... 42

Shrimp And Pineapple Ceviche 44

Tilapia Ceviche 46

Mahi Mahi Ceviche 48

Avocado Shrimp Ceviche.. 50

Overnight Ceviche 52

Fresh Tuna Ceviche... 54

Halibut-Mango Ceviche... 55

Peruvian Ceviche... 57

Soups... 59

Roasted Pumpkin-Apple Soup.. 59

Christmas-Colored Bell Pepper And Tortellini Soup................. 61

Two-Pea Soup With Ham 63

Potatoes 65

Parmesan-Romano Scalloped Potatoes...................................... 65

Elegant Twice-Baked Cheesy Potatoes...................................... 67

Make-Ahead Individual Mashed Potato Rounds........................ 69

Sweet Potatoes 71

Three-Cheese-Stuffed Sweet Potatoes....................................... 71

Sage-And-Pecan-Topped Sweet Potato Casserole With
Toasted Marshmallows.. 73

Tapas-Inspired Two-Potato Tots 76

Pasta 78

Toasty Parmesan-Cheddar Mac And Cheese 78

Creamy Chicken Alfredo Casserole 80

Cruciferous Vegetables 82

Potato-Broccoli Bake..82

Red-Wine-Infused Cabbage And Apples 84

Miscellaneous 86

Tangerine Rice Pilaf..86

Sage-Scented Sausage Stuffing 88

Creamy Corn Spoon Bread 90

Skillet Cornbread 92

Dilled Onion Cheese Balls 94

Cheddar Barbecue Meatloaf...96

Italian Mini Meatloaf Muffins 98

Refrigerator Recipes...100

Pickled Peaches..100

Smoky Cheddar Steak Fries From Scratch......................................102

Loaded Mashed Potato Casserole 104

Pecan Brown Bread Stuffing With Apples And Cherries 106

Oyster And Wild Rice Casserole..108

Squash Gratin With Poblanos & Cream...110

Smoky Creamed Kale 112

Mixed Green Salad With Grapefruit & Cranberries 114

Part 2 116

Crockpot Mushrooms 117

Crusty Herb Potato Wedges 117

Delicious Homemade Orange Zest Kale 118

Divine French Fries 119

Down South Pinto Beans 120

Easiest Asparagus Recipe 121

Easiest Corn On The Cob 122

Easy Cheesy Potatoes 123

Easy Chinese Broccoli 124

Easy Fried Zucchini 124

Easy Garlic Green Beans 125

Easy German Red Cabbage 126

Easy Glazed Carrots 127

Easy Italian Grilled Zucchini 128

Easy Lime Shredded Brussels Sprouts 129

Easy Marinated Brussels Sprouts 129

Easy Masala Hash Browns 130

Easy Pineapple Bake 131

Easy Polish Noodles 132

Easy Potato Dumplings 133

Easy Pressure Cooker Potatoes 134

Easy Roasted Broccoli...135

Easy Roasted Cabbage...136

Easy Roasted Cauliflower..136

Easy Savoy Cabbage..138

Easy Sour Cream Scalloped Potatoes.......................................139

Easy Southern Sweet Potato Casserole....................................140

Emmas Humongous Yorkshire Puddings.................................140

Escalloped Pineapple...142

Falafelcrusted Cauliflower..143

Fresh Cranberry Sauce..144

Fried Brussels Sprouts..145

Fried Buttered Noodles...146

Fried Cabbage...147

Fried Kimchi...147

Fried Yellow Squash...148

Frugal Fried Green Tomatoes...149

Garlic Butter Acorn Squash..150

Garlic Roasted Broccoli..151

German Kohlrabi In Cream Sauce..152

Gingered Swiss Chard...153

Glazed Rutabagas..154

Gourmet Wasabi Grits..155

Gramas Peppery Parsnips...156

Grandmas Armenian Rice Pilaf...157

Grilled Beets With Feta 158

Grilled Broccolimy Kids Beg For Broccoli.............................159

Grilled Butternut Squash...160

Grilled Butternut Squash With Sage 160

Grilled Cabbage With Bacon 161

Grilled Cinnamon Toast...163

Grilled Foilwrapped Potatoes 164

Grilled Parmesan Asparagus 165

Grilled Romaine..166

Grilled Salt And Pepper Bread 166

Grilled Zucchini Slices...168

Ham And Potato Casserole Easy And Economical 169

Homemade Dumplings..170

Honey Dijon Brussels Sprouts 171

Honey Ginger Green Beans..172

Honey Roasted Carrots With Cumin.......................................172

Honey Roasted Sweet Potatoes...173

Honey Soy Sweet Potatoes 174

Honey Vanilla Grilled Sweet Potatoes....................................175

How To Make Farinata 176

Instant Pot Corn On The Cob..177

Instant Pot Easy Maple Syrup Applesauce.............................178

Instant Pot Mashed Potatoes..180

Jacobs Roasted Broccoli..181

Jalapeno Creamed Corn 182

Jicama Zebra Fries..183

Josephs Best Easy Bacon Recipe...183

Kingombo Patatas...185

Lazy Green Peas..186

Lemon Honey Glazed Carrots 187

Lemonglazed Carrots..188

Part 1

Introduction

When I am creating my menu for a big dinner or an intimate gathering, the first item I figure out is the main course and then proper side dishes. The food you serve your guests as they sit down at the dinner table can set the tone for the rest of the meal, especially if thematic. When I am looking for unique side dish ideas, I turn to my tried-and-true ceviche recipes for satisfying and delicious treats my guests will love. From bass to tuna, these 30 dishes will delight and amaze your friends and family, especially when served with a Mexican-inspired beverage and some tostada shells. The light and flaky texture of this delectable starter makes it perfect for dipping. Serve with soft butter crackers or a crisp saltine and you probably won't have very much left when the main course rolls around.

Conch Ceviche With Pineapple

The fresh pineapple adds a lovely zing to the taste of this simple ceviche. Serve this with some tostada shells for scooping or some saltine crackers.

Preparation Time:15 minutes

Servings:8

Ingredients

- 32 ounces fresh conch, removed from shell
- ½ peeled and cored pineapple, chopped
- 4 ounces water
- Juice from 2 lemons
- 8 ounces fresh cilantro, chopped
- 1 medium chopped onion
- 1 medium chopped tomato
- A   pinch   of   salt

Directions

1. Trim and peel the conch then cut into ½" cubes.

2. Combine conch with the rest of the ingredients and stir gently. Let the ceviche sit for 1 hour before serving.

American Ceviche

The taste of the Clamato cocktail is delicious and goes well with a grilled steak and a Caesar. I like to serve this with some freshly baked bread and soft butter.

Preparation Time:60 minutes

Servings:20

Ingredients

- 16 ounces cooked peeled and deveined medium shrimp
- 16 ounces imitation crabmeat, cut into 1" pieces
- 5 diced tomatoes
- 3 peeled and pitted avocados, diced
- 1 peeled English cucumber, cut into small pieces
- 1 diced red onion
- 1 chopped bunch cilantro
- 4 juiced limes
- 2 seeded jalapeno peppers, finely diced
- 2 pressed garlic cloves
- 64 ounces bottle Clamato cocktail
- A pinch of salt and ground black pepper

Directions

1. Combine all ingredients except for Clamato cocktail in an airtight container. Stir until combined. Pour Clamato juice over the mixture, stir and seal the container. Chill in the refrigerator overnight. Season with salt and pepper and stir ceviche well before serving.

Ecuador Ceviche

You can barbecue sauce or salsa instead of ketchup if you want to experiment with different flavours. I like to serve this Ceviche with a fish meal featuring a lemony sauce and some grilled asparagus.

Preparation Time: 20 minutes

Servings: 9

Ingredients

- 2 large sliced Spanish onions
- 1 large ripe tomato
- 4 ounces olive oil
- 6 ounces freshly squeezed lemon juice
- 32 ounces canned oysters
- 1 diced large ripened tomato
- 3 chopped green onions
- 3 ounces ketchup
- 1/2 teaspoon soy sauce
- 1/2 teaspoon garlic salt
- 1 ounce fresh parsley, chopped
- 1/2 teaspoon white sugar

- A pinch of salt

Directions

1. Place onions in a pan and pour just enough water to cover. Turn heat to medium and bring to a simmer. Cook for 5 minutes until onion is just softened. Remove pan from heat and drain. Rinse onion in cold water.

2. With a sharp knife, make an X in the bottom and top of the tomato so it just breaks the skin.

3. Put the tomato in the same pan and pour in enough water to cover. Turn heat up to medium and simmer for 5 minutes until skin starts to peel.

4. Remove tomato from the pan and rinse in cold water. Gently peel skin off the tomato and transfer to a food processor. Puree until smooth.

5. In a large glass bowl, mix onions, oil and lemon juice. Add oysters, tomato puree, diced tomato, onions and soy sauce and stir well.

6. Season with garlic, parsley, sugar and salt before serving.

Crawfish, Crab And Shrimp Ceviche

This seafood features a seafood medley that tastes amazing when drizzled with some melted butter. Serve this on the side with some fresh salad and corn on the cob.

Preparation Time: 20 minutes

Servings: 9

Ingredients

- 8 ounces cleaned crawfish tail meat, cooked
- 8 ounces jumbo lump crabmeat
- 8 ounces peeled and deveined cooked shrimp
- 4 ounces lime juice
- 4 ounces ketchup
- 1 ounce hot pepper sauce
- 1 ounce olive oil
- 2 ½ ounces cilantro, chopped
- 4 ounces red onion diced (1/4" pieces)
- 8 ounces peeled and seeded cucumber, diced
- 8 ounces jicama, diced
- 1 seeded jalapeno chile pepper, minced
- A pinch of salt

- 1 large diced avocado

Directions

1. Check the crawfish, crab and shrimp for leftover shells and combine in a large glass bowl.

2. Pour lime juice over the seafood and mix gently so the crabmeat doesn't break up.

3. Cover the bowl and chill for 1-2 hours.

4. In the meantime, combine ketchup, oil and hot pepper sauce in another bowl. Add cilantro, red onion, diced cucumber, jicama and diced jalapeno and stir well.

5. Season with salt and fold the ketchup mixture into the chilled seafood. Place back in the refrigerator until ready to serve and top with avocado before serving.

Moroccan Spiced Sea Bass Ceviche

This ceviche is so good it deserves a main dish on its own. Serving this recipe with some crackers or a fresh baguette slice.

Preparation Time:20 minutes

Servings:6

Ingredients

- 1/3 ounce harissa
- 4 ounces unsweetened coconut milk
- 4 ounces freshly squeezed lemon juice
- 2 ounces freshly squeezed lime juice
- 2 ounces freshly squeezed orange juice
- 32 ounces diced Atlantic sea bass
- 2 ounces finely chopped red onion
- 1 teaspoon fresh ginger root, minced
- 1 ounce extra-virgin olive oil
- 1 ounce Moroccan preserved lemon, chopped
- ½ ounce lightly toasted caraway seed, crushed
- 1/2 teaspoon cumin, ground
- 1 ounce fresh chervil, chopped

11

- A pinch of kosher salt

Directions

1. Whisk Harissa, coconut milk and citrus juices together in a large glass bowl. Stir in the rest of the ingredients except for the kosher salt until well blended. Press down on the mixture so there is a layer of liquid on the top.

2. Cover bowl and chill for 3-4 hours until fish is white.

3. Season with kosher salt before serving.

Shrimp Ceviche With Coconut Milk

The coconut milk adds a mild sweet taste to this ceviche that complements the flavour of the shrimp. Serve this delectable dish with some lime juice and crackers.

Preparation Time:20 minutes

Servings:8

Ingredients

- 1 seeded lemon, cut in half
- 1 head garlic, cut in half
- 3 Turkish bay leaves
- 8 whole black peppercorns
- ½ ounce kosher salt
- 24 ounces large shrimp, peeled and deveined
- 16 ounces coconut milk
- 4 ounces lime juice
- 2 thinly sliced serrano chile peppers
- 1/2 chopped bunch cilantro
- 1 thinly sliced red onion
- 8 sprigs cilantro

- 1 fresh lime, cut into 8 wedges

Directions

1. In a large saucepan, squeeze juice out of the lemon halves and add the lemons. Stir in garlic, bay leaves, peppercorns and salt. Fill the pan up halfway with water.

2. Bring to a boil and add shrimp. Stir shrimp and remove pan from heat.

3. Leave shrimp in the hot for 5 minutes until white. Drain. Transfer shrimp to a baking sheet and chill for 30 minutes in the refrigerator.

4. Add coconut milk, lime juice, peppers, cilantro and onion in a wooden or glass bowl (not metal) and stir well. Season with salt.

5. Cut cold shrimp in half along the length and add to the coconut milk mixture. Cover bowl and chill for 30 minutes. Garnish with cilantro and lime wedges before serving.

Tomato Shrimp Ceviche

 I love the combination of tomato and shrimp flavours in this ceviche. This dish goes nicely with some baked white fish with tomato-based sauce.

Preparation Time:30 minutes

Servings:12

Ingredients

- 1 peeled medium cucumber, diced
- 1 large diced avocado
- 6 ounces red onion, diced
- 6 ounces green onion, chopped
- 24 ounces small shrimp, cooked
- 15 ounces tomato sauce
- 6 ounces tomato paste
- 4 ounces water
- 1/3 ounce salt
- 1 teaspoon pepper
- 1 teaspoon garlic salt
- Frank's hot sauce

- A pinch of salt

Directions

Mix diced cucumber, diced avocado, onions and shrimp in a large bowl until well combined. Add tomato sauce, paste and water to the mixture and mix well. If needed, add more water. Season with the rest of the ingredients to taste. Cover bowl and chill for 1 hour.

Basic Ceviche

This traditional ceviche recipe tastes amazing with some steamed vegetables and melted butter. Serve this with steak or fish as an entrée.

Preparation Time: 20 minutes

Servings: 8

Ingredients

- 16 ounces halibut, cut into bite-size pieces
- 4 ounces lime juice
- 1 large seeded tomato, diced
- 1 chopped bunch fresh cilantro
- 2 ½ ounces green bell pepper, diced
- 2 ½ ounces green onion, chopped
- 1 chopped jalapeno pepper
- 4 minced cloves garlic
- A pinch of salt and ground black pepper

Directions

1. On a large flat dish, arrange fish and pour lime juice over top.

2. Chill for 3-4 hours until fish is tender and opaque. Drain.

3. Combine the rest of the ingredients in a large bowl. Stir fish into the mixture, cover the bowl and chill for 1-2 hours before serving.

Clamato Shrimp Ceviche

This ceviche tastes best cold with some curled tortilla chips for dipping or some saltines. Serve this with a crisp green salad and some corn on the cob.

Preparation Time:20 minutes

Servings:4

Ingredients

- 32 ounces cooked shrimp
- 1 small thinly sliced red onion
- 1 fresh seeded jalapeno chile, minced
- 1 peeled and seeded cucumber, thinly sliced
- 1/2 bunch finely chopped cilantro
- 2 juiced limes
- 4 ounces Clamato Cocktail

Directions

1. Mix cooked shrimp, sliced onion, minced jalapeno, cucumber and chopped cilantro in a large bowl.

2. Add lime juice and Clamato cocktail and toss to combine. Cover bowl and chill for 1 hour before serving.

Simple Ceviche

This ceviche recipe is simple to make and lovely to serve with some freshly grilled ribs and mixed vegetables. I like to have some tortilla scoops on the table with salsa for dipping.

Preparation Time:20 minutes

Servings:5

Ingredients

- 16 ounces flaked imitation crabmeat
- 3 diced plum tomatoes
- 4 ounces fresh cilantro, chopped
- 2 chopped serrano chile peppers
- 1 chopped green onion
- 6 ounces fresh lime juice
- a pinch salt and ground black pepper

Directions

Mix all ingredients except for lime juice, salt and pepper in a large bowl and combine well.

Pour lime juice on the mixture and toss gently to combine. Season with salt and pepper before serving.

Shiitake Mushroom Ceviche

My favourite Mexican hot sauce is Cholula because of the authentic flavour, but you can use any other brand you like. The mushrooms in this recipe are plump and juicy when you take your first bite.

Preparation Time:20 minutes

Servings:2

Ingredients

- 8 ounces fresh shiitake mushrooms
- 1 chopped tomato
- 1/2 chopped onion
- 9 pitted and chopped green olives
- 1/2 teaspoon oregano, dried
- Juice from 1/2 orange
- 1 juiced lime
- 1 ounce ketchup
- ½ ounce Mexican-style hot sauce
- ¼ ounce apple cider vinegar
- A pinch of salt

Directions

1. Boil lightly salted water in a large stockpot and cook mushrooms in boiling water for 1 minute. Drain and rinse in cold water. Set mushrooms aside for 10 minutes.

2. Chop boiled mushrooms and transfer to a glass bowl. Stir in tomato, onion, green olives and oregano.

3. In a separate bowl, mix the rest of the ingredients except for salt until well combined. Pour mixture over mushrooms and season with salt. Mix gently and chill for 30 minutes before serving.

Easy Cauliflower Ceviche

I love the way the cauliflower tastes in this delicious vegetarian ceviche. If you are looking for some protein in this dish, you can add some imitation crabmeat.

Preparation Time:20 minutes

Servings:8

Ingredients

- 1 large head cauliflower
- 4 peeled carrots, finely chopped
- 3 large seeded Roma tomatoes, chopped
- 1 small white finely chopped onion
- 8 chopped sprigs cilantro
- 1 1/2 juiced limes
- salt to taste
- 1 peeled and pitted avocado, sliced

Directions

1. Fill a pan with a steamer insert with water to just below the insert. Heat water on medium high and bring to a boil. Place cauliflower in the steamer insert, cover and steam for 7-8

minutes. Remove cauliflower from heat and when cool enough to handle, finely chop

2. Combine the rest of the ingredients except for lime juice, salt and avocado in a large bowl with the boiled cauliflower. Pour lime juice on top of the mixture and season with salt.

3. Cover the bowl and chill for 1 hour. Serve topped with avocado.

Raw Vegetable Ceviche

This ceviche goes well with a vegetarian entrée and some fresh pita bread on the side. Try this with some tostada shells or tortilla scoops for dipping.

Preparation Time:20 minutes

Servings:18

Ingredients

- 1 head cauliflower, chopped into florets
- 3 peeled carrots, finely chopped
- 3 seeded Roma tomatoes, chopped
- 4 ounces sliced white mushrooms
- 1 small finely chopped onion
- 2 ounces fresh cilantro, chopped
- A pinch of salt
- 2 juiced limes
- 18 tostada shells
- 2 peeled and pitted avocados, thinly sliced

Directions

1. In large glass bowl, mix cauliflower florets, chopped carrots, chopped tomatoes, white mushrooms, onions and chopped cilantro.

2. Pour lime juice over top of the mixture and season with salt.

3. Mix gently to combine, cover and chill for 1-2 hours.

4. Serve ceviche on tostada shells with sliced avocado

Carrot Ceviche

When you are looking for a nice side dish that doesn't contain meat, then this carrot ceviche complements any type of meal. Serve as suggested on some tostada shells or with some crackers for dipping.

Preparation Time:25 minutes

Servings:8

Ingredients

- 3 large peeled carrots, grated
- 1 large chopped tomato
- 1/2 chopped small onion
- 1 seeded serrano pepper, chopped
- 15 chopped sprigs fresh cilantro
- 4 ounces ketchup
- 2 small juiced oranges
- 1 small juiced lime
- ½ ounce Mexican-style hot sauce
- salt to taste
- 8 tostada shells

- 1 peeled and pitted avocado, cut in cubes

Directions

1. Combine carrots, tomato, onion, chopped Serrano pepper and chopped cilantro in a large bowl.

2. In another bowl, mix juices and hot sauce. Pour juice mixture over the carrot mixture and season with salt. Let the ceviche stand for 1-2 hours. Drain.

3. Serve on tostada shells with cubed avocado.

Vegan Ceviche

This simple vegan ceviche recipe complements any entrée you serve. I like to serve this with some sliced cucumber for dipping.

Preparation Time:15 minutes

Servings:6

Ingredients

- 16 ounces peeled carrots, grated
- 8 ounces onion, chopped
- 8 ounces fresh cilantro, chopped
- 1 seeded serrano pepper, chopped
- 3 juiced limes
- 1 ½ ounces ketchup
- A   pinch   of   salt

Directions

Combine carrots, onion, cilantro, and serrano pepper in a glass bowl. Stir in lime juice and ketchup. Season with salt and set aside for 30 minutes.

Quick Mushroom Ceviche

This quick and easy recipe is a great addition for any dinner table. Serve this ceviche with some lemon juice drizzled over the avocado for extra tang.

Preparation Time:15 minutes

Servings:6

Ingredients

- 6 drained jars sliced mushrooms, 4 ounces each
- 1 small chopped white onion
- 4 ounces cilantro leaves, chopped
- 4 ounces ketchup
- 3 juiced limes
- A pinch of salt
- 2 peeled and pitted avocados, chopped

Directions

1.Mix sliced mushrooms, chopped onion and chopped cilantro leaves in a glass bowl. Stir in ketchup and lime and season with salt.

2.Place in refrigerator for 1 hour. Top with chopped avocado before serving.

Ceviche With Jalapenos And Red Onions

This recipe hits the spot when you want a spicy starter for your meal. For an extra kick, use spicy Clamato cocktail in the ingredients.

Preparation Time:45 minutes

Servings:10

Ingredients

- 48 ounces peeled and deveined raw shrimp, cut into small pieces
- 1/2 finely chopped white onion
- 14 juiced limes divided
- 1 serrano chile pepper
- 16 ounces shredded imitation crabmeat
- 3 seeded tomatoes, finely chopped
- 1 seeded cucumber, finely chopped
- 1/2 thinly sliced red onion
- 4 sliced jalapeno peppers
- 1 chopped bunch cilantro
- 4 ounces Clamato juice

- A pinch of salt and ground black pepper

Directions

1. Mix shrimp pieces, onion and half of the lime juice in a large bowl, cover with wrap and chill overnight to 12 hours. Drain and discard juices.

2. In a blender, place the other half of the lime juice with the Serrano pepper and blend until combined. Transfer mixture to a large glass bowl.

3. Add shrimp, onion and lime mixture to the large bowl along with crab, tomatoes, cucumber, onion, jalapeno and cilantro. Stir well.

4. Add Clamato and stir. Season with salt and pepper before serving.

Mexican Mango And White Fish Ceviche

Mango and white fish taste amazing in this ceviche recipe. I love to serve this dish with some crackers or cucumber slices for dipping.

Preparation Time:15 minutes

Servings:12

Ingredients

- 32 ounces white fish, cubed
- 4 juiced limes
- 1/2 juiced orange
- ½ ounce olive oil
- 1 chopped green chile pepper
- 2 cubed mangoes
- 5 chopped green onions
- 3 seeded tomatoes, chopped
- 4 ounces fresh cilantro, chopped
- A pinch of salt and ground black pepper

Directions

1. Mix the first five ingredients in a large glass bowl, cover and chill for 2 hours.

2. Stir in mango and onions, cover again and chill for another 20 minutes.

3. Fold the tomatoes and cilantro into the ceviche, season with salt and pepper and serve.

Easy Shrimp Ceviche

It doesn't get any easier than this simple shrimp ceviche recipe. Serve this dish on the side of your favourite meal with some saltines.

Preparation Time: 15 minutes

Servings: 4

Ingredients

- 1 diced cucumber
- 2 diced Roma tomatoes
- 1/2 diced medium red onion
- 2 seeded and deveined serrano peppers, diced
- 2 ounces cilantro, chopped
- 6 medium limes, divided
- ¼ ounce salt, divided
- 1/2 teaspoon ground black pepper
- 8 ounces peeled and deveined raw shrimp
- 1   small   diced   avocado

Directions

1. Mix diced cucumber, diced roma tomatoes, onion, Serrano peppers and chopped cilantro in a large bowl. Season with 1 tsp. of salt and juice from 1 lime. Mix gently and set aside to let flavours combine.

2. In a separate bowl, squeeze juice from the rest of the limes and season with salt and pepper.

3. Bring 64 ounces of water to boil in large stockpot. Boil shrimp in the water for 45 seconds and remove quickly with a slotted spoon.

4. When cool enough to handle, chop shrimp into small pieces and stir into the bowl with the lime juice, salt and pepper. Set aside for 20 minutes and combine with the cucumber mixture. Top with diced avocados before serving.

Swordfish, Squid And Halibut Ceviche

This seafood medley is a triple-threat and tastes outstanding with some expertly grilled steak and sautéed mushrooms. I love serving this ceviche with some roasted red peppers on top.

Preparation Time:30 minutes

Servings:16

Ingredients

- 16 ounces swordfish, cut into bite-sized pieces
- 16 ounces halibut, cut into bite-sized pieces
- 16 ounces squid, cut into thin rings
- 3 juiced limes
- 1 chopped bunch cilantro
- 4 ounces Bloody Mary mix
- 4 ounces pimento-stuffed green olives, chopped
- 4 ounces black olives, chopped
- 4 ounces yellow onion, chopped
- 4 ounces pimento peppers, chopped
- 4 ounces canned jalapeno peppers, diced
- 2 ounces frozen corn kernels

- 2 ounces frozen peas
- ½ ounce cumin seeds
- 1 teaspoon Worcestershire sauce
- ½ ounce cumin, ground

Directions

1. Place seafood pieces in a Ziploc bag and pour in lime juice. Gently squeeze the bag to coat, squeeze out any excess air and seal. Place bag in the refrigerator overnight.

2. Pour mixture from the Ziploc bag into a large glass bowl. Stir in the rest of the ingredients except for the cumin until well combined. Sprinkle ceviche with cumin before serving.

Vegan Ceviche Ii

This recipe is another vegan starter that goes well with a crisp salad and a tofu entrée. Use some carrots spears or cucumber slices to dip.

Preparation Time:20 minutes

Servings:4

Ingredients

- 8 ounces water
- 8 ounces vegetable broth
- 8 ounces quinoa
- 4 ripe avocados, cut in cubes
- 20 ounces cherry tomatoes, cut in quarters
- 24 ounces dinosaur kale, chopped
- 2 cucumbers, cut into ½" cubes
- 3 thinly sliced scallions
- 1 seeded jalapeno pepper, minced
- 1 ounce fresh cilantro, minced
- 1 juiced lemon
- ¼ ounce salt

Directions

1. Pour water, broth and quinoa into a large saucepan and bring mixture to a boil.

2. Reduce heat to medium low and cover the pan. Let quinoa simmer for 20 minutes until liquid has been absorbed and quinoa is tender.

3. Remove pan from heat and uncover. Let the quinoa sit for 5 minutes.

4. On a baking sheet, spread quinoa in an even layer and chill for 1 hour.

5. Mix quinoa with the rest of the ingredients in a large bowl until well combined and serve.

Shrimp Ceviche With Ketchup

My daughter loves this dish because ketchup is one of her favourite foods and it tastes great. Serve this with a sandwich or light dinner.

Preparation Time:45 minutes

Servings:4

Ingredients

- 16 ounces water
- A pinch of salt
- 16 ounces peeled and deveined raw medium shrimp
- 4 ounces salt
- 1 sliced red onion
- 4 juiced limes, divided
- ½ ounce corn oil
- 48 ounces fresh orange juice
- 24 ounces ketchup
- 1 ounce fresh parsley, chopped
- 1 ounce fresh cilantro, chopped
- 1 ounce fresh dill, chopped

Directions

1. Bring lightly salted water to a boil in a pan on medium high heat. Stir shrimp into the boiling water for 1 minute and turn off heat. Cook shrimp until light red with a slight curve.

2. Remove shrimp from pan with a strainer and place in a large bowl. Reserve water in the pan.

3. Mix 4 ounces of salt, onion and juice from 2 limes in a separate bowl. Stir mixture and let the ingredients stand for 1 hour.

4. Rinse onions in water and transfer them to another serving bowl.

5. Add cooked shrimp to the onions, followed by the rest of the ingredients except for reserved cooking water. Stir in 4 ounces of cooking water from the pan or more if sauce is too thick.

6. Chill for 1-2 hours before serving.

Shrimp And Pineapple Ceviche

Pineapple adds a lovely tangy flavour to this shrimp ceviche that tastes amazing when scooped up in a tortilla chip. I like to serve this starter with some pineapple slices decoratively placed on top.

Preparation Time:30 minutes

Servings:4

Ingredients

- 16 ounces cooked shrimp meat, chopped
- 8 ounces red bell pepper, chopped
- 8 ounces fresh pineapple, chopped
- 1 peeled and pitted avocado, chopped
- 1/2 finely chopped red onion
- 1/2 chopped bunch cilantro
- 1 minced clove garlic
- 1 minced serrano pepper
- 2 juiced limes
- A pinch of salt and pepper

Directions

Combine all ingredients together in a large bowl and stir until thoroughly incorporated. Cover the bowl and chill for 1-2 hours before serving.

Tilapia Ceviche

The mild flavour of tilapia makes this ceviche perfect for any entrée. Serve this beside some grilled zucchini and fresh dinner rolls.

Preparation Time:20 minutes

Servings:15

Ingredients

- 8 tilapia fillets, chopped into small pieces
- 1 large tomato, diced finely
- 1 finely diced large red onion
- 15 juiced limes
- 2 peeled and seeded cucumbers, finely diced
- 1/2 bunch cilantro, finely chopped
- A   pinch   of   salt   and   pepper

Directions

1. Place tilapia in a large bowl and pour lime juice on the fish until covered.

2. Stir in tomato, onion and diced cucumber to the tilapia mixture in the bowl

3. Place ceviche in the refrigerator for 1-2 hours to overnight and serve.

Mahi Mahi Ceviche

This ceviche tastes best after the flavours have had a chance to blend overnight. Serve this starter with some crackers and a splash of orange juice.

Preparation Time:30 minutes

Servings:6

Ingredients

- 12 ounces diced mahi mahi fillets
- 2 ½ ounces fresh lime juice
- 2 ½ ounces fresh lemon juice
- ½ ounce jalapeno pepper, minced
- 1/2 teaspoon salt
- a pinch oregano, dried
- a pinch cayenne pepper
- 4 ounces avocados, diced
- 4 ounces cucumber, peeled, seeded and diced
- 4 ounces orange segments, diced
- 4 ounces fresh chives, chopped
- 1 ounce sliced radishes
- ½ ounce cilantro, chopped

- ½ ounce olive oil

Directions

1. In a large bowl, combine fish fillets, juices, jalapeno, salt, oregano and cayenne and stir well.

2. Press down on the mahi mahi to completely cover in the liquid. Cover bowl with wrap and press down on the plastic so it is touching the mahi mahi.

3. Chill overnight.

4. Stir in the rest of the ingredients to the chilled fish mixture until completely coated. Season with salt and serve.

Avocado Shrimp Ceviche

This dish is a meal on its own, or you can serve it as a starter with some extra Worcestershire sauce and lime wedges. I like to splash some hot sauce on top before digging in.

Preparation Time:90 minutes

Servings:4

Ingredients

- 32 ounces peeled and deveined large shrimp, chopped
- 6 ounces fresh lime juice
- 5 diced plum tomatoes
- 1 chopped white onion
- 4 ounces fresh cilantro, chopped
- ½ ounce Worcestershire sauce
- ½ ounce ketchup
- 1 teaspoon Frank's hot sauce
- A pinch of salt and pepper
- 1 peeled and pitted avocado, diced
- 16 saltine crackers

Directions

1. Stir shrimp and lime juice in a large bowl until seafood is coated. Let the mixture stand for 3-5 minutes until shrimp are opaque.

2. Stir in tomatoes, onion and cilantro, cover the bowl and chill for 1-2 hours.

3. Remove shrimp from the refrigerator and stir in the rest of the ingredients except for avocado and saltines.

4. Serve ceviche in small glasses topped with diced avocado and saltines on the side.

Overnight Ceviche

If you are not in a hurry to get your side dish on the table, then let this ceviche mellow in the fridge overnight. I promise the wait will be worth it when you taste the results.

Preparation Time:15 minutes

Servings:6

Ingredients

- 16 ounces peeled and deveined raw shrimp, diced
- 4 juiced limes
- 4 seeded plum tomatoes, diced
- 1/2 finely diced yellow onion
- 1 peeled and seeded cucumber, diced
- 4 seeded serrano peppers, minced
- A pinch of salt and pepper
- 12 tostada shells
- Frank's hot sauce to taste

Directions

1. Mix shrimp with enough lime juice to cover in a large bowl. Add the rest of the ingredients except for the tostadas and hot sauce. Stir well, cover and chill for 1-2 hours.

2. Serve ceviche on tostada shells with hot sauce to taste.

Fresh Tuna Ceviche

I have tried this ceviche with fresh tuna and swordfish to delicious results. If you are lucky enough to have a grocery store that serves this fresh, then the extra cost is worth it.

Preparation Time:25 minutes

Servings:4

Ingredients

- 12 ounces sashimi grade tuna, cut in ½" cubes
- 3/4 bunch thinly sliced green onions
- 1/2 finely diced medium onion
- 1/3 ounce fresh ginger root, minced
- 1 seeded jalapeno pepper, minced
- 2 ounces lemon juice
- 1/4 teaspoon soy sauce

Directions

1.Mix all ingredients together in a large bowl, cover and chill overnight.

2.Serve and enjoy!

Halibut-Mango Ceviche

Mango adds a lovely tangy taste to this ceviche that pairs well with a fruit salad and some fresh bread. I like to serve this ceviche when I am making white fish or tilapia on the barbecue.

Preparation Time:45 minutes

Servings:6

Ingredients

- 24 ounces boneless and skinless halibut, cubed (1/2")
- 2 ½ ounce fresh lime juice
- 2 ounces fresh lemon juice
- 2 ounces tequila
- 3 seeded jalapeno chile peppers, minced
- 1 peeled and seeded mango, diced
- 1 seeded green bell pepper, finely chopped
- 4 ounces Vidalia onion, finely chopped
- 4 ounces red onion, finely chopped
- 1 peeled and seeded mango, diced
- 1/2 bunch fresh cilantro, chopped

- 2 ounces fresh parsley, chopped
- 1   teaspoon   salt

Directions

1. In a large glass bowl, mix fish, juices, tequila, jalapeno and mango. Cover the bowl and chill for 2 hours.

2. Stir in bell pepper and onions until well combined. Cover again and chill for another 30 minutes.

3. Fold in the rest of the ingredients and add more salt to taste before serving.

Peruvian Ceviche

The hard-boiled eggs add a lovely flavour to this ceviche recipe that you will adore. You can use bottled juices for the ingredients if you don't have a juicer or fresh fruit.

Preparation Time:25 minutes

Servings:4

Ingredients

- 4 ounces freshly squeezed lemon juice
- 2 ounces freshly squeezed lime juice
- 2 ounces freshly squeezed orange juice
- 1 teaspoon fresh ginger, grated
- 1 ounce extra virgin olive oil
- 16 ounces fresh sea bass fillets, cut ¼" thick
- 2 ounces fresh cilantro, chopped
- 1 thinly sliced onion
- 2 peeled and pitted avocados, cut in cubes
- A pinch of salt and pepper
- 4 hard-boiled eggs, cut in quarters

Directions

1. In a large glass bowl, mix juices, ginger and oil. Toss bass in the liquid to coat. Cover the bowl and chill for 2-3 hours until fish is opaque and white.

2. Stir in the rest of the ingredients except for the eggs. Top with egg wedges before serving.

Soups

Roasted Pumpkin-Apple Soup

Serves: 6

Make-Ahead: Freeze up to 3 months, or refrigerate up to 3 days

Feel free to omit the hazelnut and hazelnut oil garnish. You can top with any chopped nut you desire...or don't top with any at all. A swirl of cream before serving makes for a pretty contrast if you don't want to use hazelnut oil.

2 large sweet-tart apples, cored, and cut each into 8 equal wedges

2 pounds pie pumpkin or butternut squash, peeled, deseeded, and chopped into chunks

2 tablespoons extra virgin olive oil

Salt, to taste

Freshly ground pepper, to taste

1/2 tablespoon chopped fresh sage

4 cups chicken or vegetable stock

TO SERVE (optional)

3 tablespoons chopped hazelnuts or pumpkin seeds

1 tablespoon hazelnut oil

Preheat oven to 425°F.

Toss apples, pumpkin, extra virgin olive oil, salt, and pepper together in a large bowl.

Transfer to a rimmed baking sheet, spreading the apple and pumpkin out in a single layer. Bake for 20 to 30 minutes, or

59

until pumpkin is tender. Add sage to pan, stirring to evenly distribute. Roast for 15 minutes, or until pumpkin is slightly brown. Stir once halfway through baking. Remove from the oven, and let cool for 20 minutes.

Transfer in batches to a blender, and blend with stock until smooth. Pour mixture into a Dutch oven or soup pot. Heat through, stirring frequently. Turn off heat, and let cool completely.

To Freeze or Refrigerate: Transfer into an airtight plastic container. Label with name and date. Refrigerate up to 3 days, or freeze up to 3 months.

To Serve

Thaw in the refrigerator for 1 to 2 days before serving, if frozen.

Pour thawed or refrigerated soup into a microwave-safe bowl. Cover, and microwave on High until thoroughly heated, stirring every 2 minutes to evenly distribute heat; time depends on your oven's wattage. Alternatively, soup can also be reheated on the stovetop. Pour soup into a soup pot over medium-low heat. Simmer soup for 30 minutes, or until heated through, stirring frequently.

Ladle into soup bowls. Garnish with hazelnuts and hazelnut oil, if using.

Christmas-Colored Bell Pepper And Tortellini Soup

Serves: 8

Make-Ahead: Freeze up to 1 month

No cooking required until you're ready to eat! Simply freeze the combined chunky ingredients ahead of time, and you'll have soup in no time. Reheat day is just as easy. The frozen vegetables and pasta are not thawed before making the soup.

Fresh basil makes this especially flavorful and pretty, though it can be hard to get during the holidays. If you can't find good fresh basil in winter, substitute finely shredded escarole or finely chopped arugula; toss into the soup pot with the frozen vegetables and pasta. While neither, of course, has the flavor of basil, either will add its own flavor and color.

2 (14.5 ounce) cans Italian-style stewed tomatoes, undrained
2 (9 ounce) packages refrigerated three-cheese tortellini
1 small red bell pepper, chopped
1 small green bell pepper, chopped
TO SERVE

2 1/2 cups water
2 (14.5 ounce) cans chicken broth
Salt, to taste
2/3 cup snipped fresh basil (optional in winter; see headnote)
Grated Parmesan cheese (optional)

To Freeze: Combine tomatoes, tortellini, and bell peppers in a freezer-safe bag. Seal the bag after removing all the air. Label with name and date. Freeze for up to 1 month.

To Serve: Bring the water and broth to a boil in a large soup pot over medium heat. Add the frozen contents of the bag to the boiling water. After water boils again, cover pot with a lid, and simmer for 30 minutes, stirring occasionally, or until soup is heated through and the frozen vegetables and pasta are completely thawed and evenly hot. Stir in salt, and add basil if using; allow basil to wilt. Ladle into soup bowls. Garnish with Parmesan, if using.

Two-Pea Soup With Ham

Serves: 12

Make-Ahead: Freeze up to 2 months, or refrigerate up to 3 days

The aromatics are lightly roasted in this flavorful ham-and-pea soup. Both split peas and fresh-frozen peas are used for a more complex pea flavor and texture.

4 medium carrots, cut into 1" pieces

2 large onions, halved and cut into thick slices

4 stalks celery, cut into 1" pieces

6 cloves garlic, peeled

2 tablespoons olive oil

4 pounds ham hocks

12 cups water

1 teaspoon dried marjoram, crushed

2 cups dry split peas, rinsed and drained

1/2 teaspoon pepper

2 (16 ounce) packages frozen green peas

2/3 cup chopped fresh flat-leaf parsley

Salt, to taste (optional)

1/4 cup fresh-squeezed lemon juice

Preheat oven to 425°F.

Toss carrots, onion, celery, and garlic with olive oil in a 13" x 9" baking dish. Distribute tossed vegetables evenly in the pan in a single layer. Bake for about 20 minutes, or until carrots are tender. Stir once halfway through baking.

Transfer vegetables into a Dutch oven or a large soup pot over medium-high heat. Add ham hocks, water, marjoram, split peas, and pepper; stir. When pot comes to a boil, lower heat, cover with a lid, and simmer for about 1 hour, or until the split peas are tender. Stir occasionally. Turn off heat. Remove ham hocks to a cutting board. Add frozen peas and parsley to pot; stir. Let cool for 20 minutes.

When ham hocks are cool enough to handle, shred some of the meat (about 1 1/2 cups); place in a zip-top freezer-safe bag; label, and date. Chop the remaining meat; reserve.

Blend soup in batches until smooth. Add the mixture back into the Dutch oven. Add lemon juice and chopped ham; stir. Taste to adjust seasoning; add more pepper or salt, if desired.

To Freeze: Place the soup into a large airtight, freezer-safe container (or several smaller ones). Label with name and date. Attach meat zip-top bag to the container. Refrigerate up 3 days, or freeze up to 2 months.

To Serve

Thaw in the refrigerator for 1 to 2 days before serving, if frozen.

Pour soup into a Dutch oven or soup pot. Simmer soup for 30 minutes, or until heated through. Taste, and adjust the seasonings if necessary.

Ladle into bowls. Scatter shredded ham on top; serve.

Potatoes

Parmesan-Romano Scalloped Potatoes

Serves: 8

Make-Ahead: Freeze up to 1 month

The gold and red skins of the potatoes make this dish feel more festive, but feel free to remove the skins if you have guests who do not like them. If you prefer a different cheese in your scalloped potatoes, feel free to substitute your favorite.

You can use the **Slab Method of Freezing**, as described in the Make-Ahead Tips section, to free up your baking dish and allow for tighter freezer packing.

2 pounds Yukon Gold potatoes, sliced with skin on

2 pounds red potatoes, sliced with skin on

4 ounces Parmesan cheese, grated (more or less to taste)

CHEESE SAUCE

1/2 cup butter

1/2 cup flour

4 cups milk

Freshly ground black pepper, to your preference

8 ounces Romano or Muenster cheese, grated

Boil potato slices until just tender but still firm. While potatoes boil, make the sauce.

Melt butter in a heavy pan over medium-low heat. Add flour and pepper, whisking to combine. When mixture starts to bubble, slowly add milk, whisking constantly to avoid lumps.

Continue whisking until mixture is slightly thickened. Add Romano or Muenster cheese, stirring until cheese is melted.

Remove potatoes from the pot when tender, and place in a large bowl. When sauce is done, pour it over the potato slices, and stir to combine. Distribute the potato-sauce mixture evenly in the bottom of a greased 13" x 9" baking dish. Sprinkle Parmesan cheese over the top.

To Freeze: Wrap tightly, label, and freeze up to 1 month.

To Serve: Thaw completely in the refrigerator 1 or 2 days before serving. Remove wrap. Bake at 350°F for 25 minutes, or until heated through.

Elegant Twice-Baked Cheesy Potatoes

Serves: 12 or more

Make-Ahead: Freeze up to 6 weeks

12 medium-to-large Yukon Gold or other yellow potatoes, scrubbed

1 teaspoon salt

1/2 teaspoon pepper

1/4 cup butter or margarine

1 teaspoon onion powder or granulated onion

Milk, as needed (see TIP)

3 cups shredded Muenster or Asiago cheese

Preheat oven to 400°F. Bake potatoes for 1 hour, or until a cake tester slides smoothly through the middle. Remove potatoes from the oven, and allow them to cool for a few minutes. Slice potatoes in half lengthwise, with the flatter two sides of the potato parallel to the cut. (This way, the potatoes will sit better on the pan when they are baked again.)

Carefully scoop out the potato pulp, leaving a 1/4" shell near the skin. Place the pulp in a bowl. Continue until pulp has been removed from all potatoes. Mash pulp with salt, pepper, onion powder, and butter; some small lumps are OK. Add a splash of milk if the mixture seems dry. Add cheese, and combine until cheese is melted and thoroughly mixed in with the potatoes. Mound potato-cheese mixture into potato shells. To Freeze: Freeze potato halves individually on a baking sheet until hard. Put the frozen halves in gallon-sized freezer bags labelled with name and date.

To Serve: Remove as many potatoes as needed (1 to 2 per person) the night before serving, and place on a plate in the refrigerator. Cover with plastic wrap so they don't dry out while thawing. When thawed, place in a shallow baking dish, and bake at 400°F for 20 minutes, or until golden brown.

TIP

You can use unflavored soy milk instead of dairy milk to add moisture.

Not-So-Elegant Twice-Baked Sriracha Potatoes Variation

Substitute Monterey Jack for the Muenster cheese (you can use pepper Jack if you like). After the cheese has just melted into the potato mixture, add 1 tablespoon of Sriracha sauce (or to taste), and blend to combine thoroughly.

VARIATIONS

- Add chopped olives or tapenade to the potato mixture after the cheese.
- Add chopped marinated artichoke hearts to the potato mixture after the cheese.
- Add chopped sun-dried tomatoes to the potato mixture after the cheese.

Make-Ahead Individual Mashed Potato Rounds

Serves: 12

Make-Ahead: Freeze up to 2 months

Mashed potatoes are my favorite side dish for any holiday...or any meal! In this make-ahead version, two types of potatoes are mashed together and formed into mounded rounds for individual serving. You can use the rounds on the spur of the moment, as they are baked from frozen!

1 1/2 pounds small russet potatoes, peeled and cut into fourths

1 1/2 pounds red or yellow potatoes, peeled and cut into fourths

1/2 cup milk

6 tablespoons butter or margarine, softened

3 eggs, beaten

1/2 teaspoon black pepper

TO SERVE

Melted butter, for brushing on tops

Boil potatoes in lightly salted water until tender, about 15 minutes. Drain water from pot. Turn off heat, and shake potatoes in pot to evaporate excess moisture. Mash potatoes in pot, adding milk to help smooth. Add butter in pieces, mashing to incorporate. You may need to add a little more milk to make the potatoes fluffy and smooth, but do not make the mixture runny or too light. Add eggs when the mixture has cooled slightly, mixing quickly to incorporate fully so the eggs don't solidify and partially cook. Stir in pepper.

To Freeze: Form potatoes into 12 mounded rounds on an ungreased cookie sheet. Freeze until firm, about 45 minutes to 1 hour. Place in an airtight freezer container or gallon-sized zip-top bags, label, and freeze. Freeze up to 2 months.

To Serve: Preheat oven to 375°F, and grease a cookie sheet. Place frozen potato rounds on the sheet. Brush each mound with melted butter. Bake 20 to 25 minutes, or until heated through.

VARIATION

Add 1/3 cup shredded blanched root vegetable (carrot, sweet potato, celeriac, parsnip, etc.) to the potato mixture just before the eggs.

Sweet Potatoes

Three-Cheese-Stuffed Sweet Potatoes

Serves: 4

Make-Ahead: Freeze up to 1 month

4 small sweet potatoes (5 to 6 ounces each), rinsed and scrubbed

1/4 cup ricotta cheese (skim OK)

4 ounces soft fresh goat cheese

1/2 cup cottage cheese (fat free OK)

Salt, to taste

Pepper, to taste

TO SERVE

2 green onions, sliced

Paprika, to taste

Pierce the sweet potatoes lightly with a fork. Microwave on High for 6 minutes, or until tender.

Remove sweet potatoes to a cutting board. When they have cooled enough to handle, halve lengthwise. Scoop out potato pulp with a spoon, leaving 1/4" shell intact; place pulp in a bowl. Remove as much pulp as possible without spoiling the shell. Set the potato shells aside.

Mash potato pulp; add ricotta cheese, goat cheese, and cottage cheese. Mix well. Add salt and pepper to taste. Spoon the sweet potato mixture into the potato shells.

Microwave each potato on High for 1 minute. Cool completely.

To Freeze: Freeze potato halves individually on a baking sheet until hard. Put the frozen halves in gallon-sized freezer bags labelled with name and date. Freeze up to 1 month.

To Serve: Thaw completely in the refrigerator 1 or 2 days before serving. When thawed, place in a shallow baking dish, and bake at 400°F for 20 minutes, or until golden brown. Garnish with green onion and paprika.

Sage-And-Pecan-Topped Sweet Potato

Casserole With Toasted Marshmallows

Serves: 8

Make-Ahead: Freeze up to 6 weeks

Who doesn't love toasted marshmallows? Up your sweet potato casserole game with mixed-in toasted marshmallows and a sweet-and-savory topping.

You can use the **Slab Method of Freezing**, as described in the Make-Ahead Tips section, to free up your baking dish and allow for tighter freezer packing.

SAGE-AND-PECAN TOPPING

1/2 cup all-purpose flour

5 tablespoons chilled butter, cut into tiny pieces

5 to 6 fresh sage leaves, finely chopped

6 tablespoons packed dark brown sugar

1 cup chopped pecans, finely chopped with some larger pieces

Zest of 1 orange, chopped

SWEET POTATOES

2 pounds sweet potatoes, scrubbed

2 tablespoons vegetable oil

1/2 cup all-purpose flour

1/4 cup butter

1/2 cup heavy cream

1/4 cup packed dark brown sugar, plus extra if required

1 teaspoon salt

1/2 teaspoon pumpkin pie spice

73

1 cup mini marshmallows, or more if desired

2 eggs, beaten

SAGE-AND-PECAN TOPPING

Combine all topping ingredients in a bowl; mix using your hands until crumbly in texture. Cover, and refrigerate while preparing rest of recipe.

SWEET POTATOES

Place the oven rack in the center of the oven. Preheat oven to 400°F.

Prick sweet potatoes using a fork, piercing about 1/4" into the flesh. Brush oil over sweet potatoes, rubbing it into the skin. Place on a baking sheet.

Bake for about 40 to 50 minutes, or until sweet potatoes are tender. Remove from oven, and let cool for at least 20 minutes. When cool enough to handle, remove and discard skins.

Place sweet potatoes in a large bowl. Add flour, butter, cream, brown sugar, salt, and pumpkin pie spice. Mash until smooth and well combined.

Carefully place oven rack in the low broiling position; switch on the broiler setting. Place marshmallows on a baking sheet in a single layer. Broil, keeping watch over marshmallows the entire time as they can burn quickly. When the marshmallows begin to sear and smoke, remove pan **immediately** from the oven.

Reduce oven temperature to 375°F.

Add toasted marshmallows to the bowl of mashed sweet potatoes, stirring with a rubber spatula until well incorporated. Taste, and add more brown sugar, salt, and/or pumpkin pie spice if desired. If more brown sugar is needed, add a tablespoon at a time, and mix well each time until the taste you desire is achieved. Add eggs, and mix until well incorporated.

To Freeze: Transfer into a greased 11" x 7" baking dish, spreading evenly. Refrigerate until well chilled. Sprinkle with reserved topping. Cover the dish with plastic wrap first and then with aluminum foil. Label with name and date. Freeze up to 6 weeks.

To Serve: Thaw in the refrigerator overnight. Remove plastic wrap and foil. Bake in a preheated oven at 350°F for about 30 minutes, or until golden on top. Let stand 5 minutes before serving.

Tapas-Inspired Two-Potato Tots

Serves: 8

Make-Ahead: Freeze up to 1 month

If you love tots, ratchet them up a few notches with this recipe! Regular and sweet potatoes combine with chorizo and olives for a tot like no other! These are individually frozen, so you can take out whatever you need—perfect for when you have unexpected company.

2 large russet potatoes, scrubbed, peeled, and chopped into large chunks (see TIP)

2 large sweet potatoes, scrubbed, peeled, and chopped into large chunks (see TIP)

4 cooked or dried chorizo links, cut into small pieces

1/2 cup roughly chopped pitted olives

1/2 cup roughly chopped sliced almonds (optional)

2 teaspoon smoked paprika

Kosher salt, to taste

TO SERVE

Canola or vegetable oil, for deep frying

Bring sweet and russet potato chunks to a boil in a large pot of salted water. Keeping the water at a low boil, continue to boil for about 5 minutes. Potatoes should not be fully cooked. Drain, and allow to cool for a few minutes.

When cool enough to handle, grate potatoes on a box grater or in a food processor. Mix the shredded potatoes together with the chorizo, olives, almonds (if using), paprika, and salt. Make small portions of the mixture into logs or balls, about the size of a commercial tot or a little larger.

To Freeze: Place tots on a tray, and freeze until firm. Transfer to a freezer bag. Label with name and date. Freeze up to a month.

To Serve: Remove tots from freezer, allowing them to thaw slightly while oil comes to temperature. Pour canola oil into a small, deep pan (around 1" to 2" tall), and heat until the oil is about 350°F. Add 4 to 5 tots, and fry until golden brown, turning a couple of times for even browning. Remove with a slotted spoon to a plate lined with paper towels. Repeat the previous step with the remaining tots. Serve hot.

TIP

If you want "dirty" loaded tots, leave potatoes unpeeled. The skin may fall off when the potatoes are boiled and will most likely fall off during grating. Gather these bits of potato peel and chop so flecks will be throughout potato mixture.

Pasta

Toasty Parmesan-Cheddar Mac And Cheese

Serves: 8 to 10

Make-Ahead: Freeze up to 1 month

This is another dish that would benefit from the **Slab Method of Freezing** mentioned in the Make-Ahead Tips section.

The recipe makes enough to fill a 13" x 9" baking dish or two 8" x 8" ones. You can choose the size dish you would like based on whether you plan to use the recipe for a large or small gathering.

Butter, for greasing baking dish(es)

1 pound elbow macaroni

6 tablespoons butter

4 tablespoons all-purpose flour

5 cups whole milk

Salt, to taste

Freshly ground black pepper, to taste

1 cup grated Parmesan cheese

1 pound cheddar cheese, grated

TO SERVE

1 cup crushed buttery crackers (like Ritz)

1/2 cup grated Parmesan cheese

Grease a 13" x 9" baking dish with butter (or two 8" x 8" ones), and set aside.

Cook the macaroni according to package directions **but for 2 minutes less** than stated. Drain, and set aside.

Place a medium-sized pot over medium heat. Melt butter, and then add flour, whisking for a couple of minutes to fully blend the two. Do not brown. Gently pour in the milk, whisking constantly to avoid lumps. Add salt and pepper. Bring to a boil, stirring constantly, until the sauce thickens. Lower the heat, and simmer for about 10 minutes, stirring occasionally.

Turn off heat, and add both cheeses. Whisk until cheese has melted into the thickened milk. Add the cheese sauce to the cooked pasta, and toss to combine thoroughly.

To Freeze: Divide the mixture into baking dishes if using more than one. Spread mixture evenly over the bottom(s). Cover dish(es) with plastic wrap first and then with aluminum foil. Label with name and date. Freeze up to 1 month.

To Serve: Thaw in refrigerator overnight. Combine crushed crackers and grated Parmesan. Remove both coverings, sprinkle the top(s) with crushed cracker mixture, and recover the dish(es) with the foil. Bake at 350 °F for 30 minutes. Remove the foil, and bake for 10 minutes, or until golden on top.

Creamy Chicken Alfredo Casserole

Serves: 10 to 12

Make-Ahead: Freeze up to 1 month, or refrigerate up to 3 days

If you have cooked chicken on hand, nothing besides the pasta is cooked on preparation day! It is mostly an assemble-and-freeze recipe. This is a great dish to have on hand even when it is not the holiday season. To keep your baking dish available for other uses, use the **Slab Method of Freezing** for this dish described in the Make-Ahead Tips section.

This makes a lot, one larger dish for The Big Day and one smaller dish perfect for a hectic night during the holiday season.

Butter or oil, for preparing dish

24 ounces uncooked penne pasta

2 (15 ounce) jars Alfredo sauce

1/2 cup chicken stock

2 (6 ounce) packages fresh baby spinach, chopped

2/3 cup refrigerated pesto

5 cups chopped cooked chicken

TO SERVE

8 ounces shredded mozzarella cheese

1/4 cup fresh basil, thinly sliced

1/2 teaspoon paprika

Grease one 13" x 9" baking dish and one 8" x 8" baking dish with a little butter or oil.

Cook penne according to package directions. Drain, and allow to cool before assembling the completed dish.

Combine Alfredo sauce and stock in a bowl; whisk well. Mix spinach and pesto in another bowl.

Spread about 2/3 cup of the Alfredo sauce mixture all over the bottom of the larger baking dish and 1/3 cup over the bottom of the smaller one. Sprinkle half the spinach mixture evenly over both pans. In a separate bowl, combine pasta, remaining Alfredo mixture, and chicken. Spread half evenly over the spinach mixture in the baking dishes. Layer remaining spinach mixture followed by remaining chicken mixture.

To Freeze: Cover the dish with plastic wrap first and then with aluminum foil. Label with name and date. Refrigerate for 2 to 3 days, or freeze up to 1 month.

To Serve: Thaw completely in the refrigerator 1 or 2 days before serving. Remove both the plastic wrap and the foil, and then recover with the foil. Bake at 375°F for about 30 minutes. Remove from oven, discard foil, and sprinkle mozzarella on top. Bake until the cheese is bubbling, about 10 minutes. Garnish with paprika and basil.

Cruciferous Vegetables

Potato-Broccoli Bake

Serves: 12

Make-Ahead: Freeze up to 1 month

For best results, pick a generic brand of hash brown cubes (not one of the big frozen potato producers), as these tend to be just potatoes with a little preservative. Don't use hash browns that have added fat/oil, as this will give an off taste to the casserole and make it greasy.

This dish is particularly ripe for experimentation. Use any type of potatoes (fries, tots, sweet potatoes). Pick any other vegetable that seems to go with potatoes and the type(s) of cheese you intend to use. Use different canned soups, or make your own thick white sauce with the star ingredient of your choice. Use just about any melty cheese combination, or make it with half melty cheese and half drier cheese. See below the recipe for some fun variations.

2 pounds frozen hash brown cubes, picked over to remove discolored ones

4 to 5 cups broccoli, chopped into bite-sized pieces

1 (10.75 ounce) can cream of onion or mushroom soup

1 (10.75 ounce) can cream of broccoli soup

2 cups milk

1 cup mild cheddar, grated

1 cup sharp cheddar, grated

Grease two 13" x 9" baking dishes. (Disposable ones work fine.)

Steam broccoli until crisp-tender. Allow to cool slightly.

Divide and spread hash brown cubes over the bottoms of the baking dishes. (Disposable ones work fine.) Distribute broccoli evenly over the potatoes.

In a medium bowl, combine soups and milk; pour evenly over the vegetables. In a small bowl, combine cheeses. Sprinkle the top of each baking dish with 1 cup of the combined cheeses.

To Freeze: Wrap each baking dish well with plastic wrap and then foil. Label, and freeze.

To Serve: Thaw completely in the refrigerator 1 or 2 days before serving. Remove wrap. Bake uncovered at 350°F for 25 to 30 minutes.

Sweet Potato-Cauliflower Variation

Substitute sweet potato fries for the hash brown cubes. Substitute roasted cauliflower for the broccoli. Omit the cream of broccoli soup, and add another can of cream of onion or mushroom soup.

VARIATIONS

- Use halved, steamed Brussels sprouts instead of broccoli.
- Use frozen winter squash cubes instead of broccoli.
- Roast the broccoli instead of steaming it.
- Use a single type of cheddar or any cheddar combination. Substitute another good melting cheese for one cup of the cheddar.

Red-Wine-Infused Cabbage And Apples

Serves: 8

Make-Ahead: Freeze up to 3 months

We all know it is good to "eat the rainbow," but in winter, our favorite red food is a shadow of its former summer self. Get your red food with this sweet-and-sour festive dish.

2 tablespoons butter

1 medium onion, finely chopped

2 apples (like Honeycrisp), peeled, cored, and diced

1 cup vegetable or chicken stock

1/2 cup red wine

1/3 cup red wine or balsamic vinegar

1/4 cup packed dark brown sugar

1 bay leaf

1/2 teaspoon salt

1/4 teaspoon pepper

1 medium red cabbage, finely shredded

2 teaspoons cornstarch

2 tablespoons cold water

Melt butter over medium heat in a medium-sized soup pot. Sauté onions and apples, stirring occasionally, until onions are translucent.

Add stock, wine, vinegar, brown sugar, bay leaf, salt, and pepper. Bring to a full boil. Stir in cabbage. Cover, turn down heat to low, and simmer, stirring occasionally, until the cabbage is tender (40 to 45 minutes). Blend cornstarch with water; stir into cabbage mixture. Cook a few minutes more until sauce is slightly thickened. Remove bay leaf. Cool completely.

To Freeze: Package in an airtight freezer-safe container or freezer bag. Label, and freeze. Freeze up to 3 months.
To Serve: Thaw completely in the refrigerator 1 or 2 days before serving. Thaw in the refrigerator in a bowl if you've saved it in bags. Reheat on over low-medium heat on the stovetop until contents are completely heated through, approximately 10 minutes.

Miscellaneous

Tangerine Rice Pilaf

Serves: 8

Make-Ahead: Freeze up to 2 months

4 1/2 cups chicken or vegetable stock

2 cups short-grain brown rice

1/4 teaspoon ground cinnamon, or to taste

2 teaspoons grated tangerine zest

2/3 cup raisins

2/3 cup almonds, sliced, toasted

TO SERVE

1 cup sliced green onion

4 tangerines, peeled and seeds removed

Bring broth to a boil in a 3-quart pot over medium heat. Stir in rice, cinnamon, and zest. Lower heat, and simmer, covered, for 45 minutes. Remove from heat, and let stand for 10 minutes, covered. Fluff rice with a fork. Add raisins and almonds; toss well.

To Freeze: Cool completely. Transfer to freezer-safe bags. Label with name and date.

To Serve: Thaw completely in the refrigerator 1 or 2 days before serving. Transfer into a microwave-safe bowl, and add green onions, stirring to combine. Microwave times vary depending on wattage, so start small and add more time as needed. Microwave for 4 minutes to start; stir, and determine how much more time might be needed. When the rice mixture is heated through, separate tangerines into segments, and cut the segments into smaller pieces. Garnish rice with tangerine pieces.

Sage-Scented Sausage Stuffing

Serves: 12

Make-Ahead: Freeze up to 3 weeks

1 (4 ounce) stick butter plus 2 tablespoons, divided use

1 1/2 pounds sweet Italian sausage, casings removed

1 large onion, chopped into 1/2" pieces

6 stalks celery, chopped into 1/2" pieces

1 1/2 tablespoons dried sage

1 1/2 tablespoons dried thyme

Kosher salt, to taste

Freshly ground black pepper, to taste

1 to 2 loaves stale bread (approximately 2 pounds total), cut into 1/2" cubes

TO SERVE

3 cups turkey or chicken stock

1 (4 ounce) stick butter plus 2 tablespoons, divided use

3 eggs

3/4 cup chopped fresh parsley

Melt 2 tablespoons butter in a large nonstick skillet over medium-high heat. When butter is melted, add sausage and brown, breaking the meat into bite-sized chunks as it cooks. Remove sausage with a slotted spoon, and place in a large bowl.

Melt 1 stick butter in the skillet. When butter is melted, add onion, celery, sage, thyme, salt, and pepper; sauté until onion becomes light brown.

Add onion-celery mixture to the sausage bowl; stir to combine. Add bread, and toss until ingredients are evenly distributed.

Let cool completely.

To Freeze: Transfer into freezer-safe bags. Label with name and date. Freeze up to 3 weeks.

To Serve

Thaw at room temperature for 30 to 40 minutes. Preheat oven to 350°F, and grease 13" x 9" baking dish

Melt 1 stick butter in stock in a saucepan placed over medium heat. Remove pan from heat.

Crack eggs into a bowl, and whisk well. Add parsley, and whisk again.

Remove stuffing from the bag, and break into smaller pieces. Place pieces in a large bowl. Pour egg mixture over stuffing, and toss well. Pour heated stock mixture into the bowl, and stir until well combined.

Transfer mixture into prepared baking dish. Dot the surface with the remaining butter. Cover the dish tightly with foil.

Bake for 50 to 60 minutes. Remove foil, and bake until the top is golden brown. Remove from oven, and let stand a few minutes before serving.

Creamy Corn Spoon Bread

Serves: 12

Make-Ahead: Freeze up to 3 weeks, or refrigerated for one day

Yes, this well-loved holiday dish can be assembled in advance to be tucked away in the freezer or refrigerator. If you try the refrigerator version, you'll be surprised the way the simple flavors meld compared to if you pop it in the oven straightaway after combining. You have the option of making two smaller spoon breads or one larger one.

6 eggs

2 cups sour cream

1 cup butter, melted and cooled

2 (15 ounce) cans whole-kernel corn, drained

2 (15 ounce) cans cream-style corn, undrained

2 (8.5 ounce) boxes store-bought corn muffin mix (Jiffy)

1 teaspoon salt

Whisk eggs in a medium-sized bowl. Stir in sour cream and butter, blending well. Add all other ingredients, and stir until thoroughly mixed.

To Refrigerate: Lightly grease a 13" x 9" baking dish or two 8" x 8" baking dishes. Spread batter evenly over the bottom(s) of the dish(es). Cover dish(es) tightly with plastic wrap. Refrigerate up to 24 hours.

To Freeze: If you plan to use this recipe for two different meals, divide batter evenly into two freezer-safe bags. If you will be using the entire recipe, pour all batter into a gallon-sized freezer-safe bag. Label with name and date. Freeze up to 3 weeks.

To Serve

If frozen, thaw completely in the refrigerator 1 or 2 days before serving. Thaw the bag in a bowl in case there are any leaks. Transfer batter into a lightly greased 13" x 9" baking dish or two 8" x 8" baking dishes.

If refrigerated, remove baking dish from refrigerator, and unwrap. Let stand at room temperature for 30 minutes.

Bake at 350°F for 40 to 50 minutes, or until center no longer jiggles.

Skillet Cornbread

Serves: 16

Make-Ahead: Freeze up to 6 months, or refrigerate up to 4 days

Creamed corn can sizes vary slightly. So long as it is close to 15 ounces, you'll be fine with this recipe and the previous one.

4 cups cornmeal

1 teaspoon baking soda

4 teaspoons baking powder

2 tablespoons sugar

2 teaspoons kosher salt

4 eggs

2 cups buttermilk

1 (15 ounce) can creamed corn

1/4 cup canola oil

Place a large cast-iron skillet in the oven, and preheat to 425°F with skillet inside.

Combine cornmeal, baking soda, baking powder, sugar, and salt in a bowl. Combine eggs, buttermilk, and creamed corn in a separate bowl; whisk well. Pour creamed corn mixture into the cornmeal mixture; combine to make a batter. If the batter is too thick, stir in a little more buttermilk.

Remove hot skillet from oven. Add oil, and swirl the skillet so that the oil spreads all over the bottom of the skillet and a little up the sides. Spoon the batter into the skillet.

Bake for 20 to 30 minutes, or until golden brown on top. Remove cornbread from skillet, and cool completely.

To Freeze or Refrigerate: Wrap tightly first in plastic wrap and then in heavy-duty aluminum foil. Label with name and date. Freeze up to 6 months, or place in the refrigerator for 2 to 4 days.

To Serve

Thaw completely, if frozen. Warm the cornbread for 30 seconds in the microwave, if desired.

Make a pretty presentation by putting the cornbread back in the skillet it was baked in, and decorate the handle with festive streamers. Cut into cornbread into wedges.

Dilled Onion Cheese Balls

Makes: 20 to 30 balls

Make-Ahead: Freeze up to 3 months

2 (8 ounce) packages cream cheese, softened

1 (4 ounce) stick butter

8 ounces Gouda cheese, finely shredded

1 teaspoon Worcestershire sauce, or to taste

2 tablespoons milk

1/4 cup fresh snipped dill (or 4 teaspoons dried dill)

1/4 cup thinly sliced green onion

TO SERVE

Assorted crackers and/or flatbread

COATINGS (use 2 or 3)

Poppy seeds

Finely snipped chives and paprika

Finely chopped Craisins® and toasted pecans

Finely crushed Cheez-Its®

Finely shredded cheddar cheese

Finely crushed tortilla chips

Finely crumbled crispy bacon

Place cream cheese, butter, and Gouda cheese in a mixing bowl. Let stand at room temperature for 30 minutes.

Add Worcestershire sauce and milk to cheese mixture. Using an electric mixer, beat at medium speed until creamy and light. Add dill and green onion, and beat until they are distributed evenly in the cream cheese mixture. Make 20 to 30 equal portions, and form each portion into a ball.

To Freeze: Place on a tray, and freeze until firm. Transfer to a freezer-safe container. Label with name and date. Freeze up to 3 months.

To Serve: Thaw completely in the refrigerator 1 day before serving. Place 2 to 3 different flavored coatings in separate small bowls. Dredge the balls in chosen coating, and serve with crackers.

Cheddar Barbecue Meatloaf

Serves: 20 to 24

Make-Ahead: Freeze up to 1 month

Meatloaf...as a side dish? The holiday sideboard typically groans with many types of dishes...so why not? This loaf is meant to be cut into small slices so that your guests can have a small slab of meatloaf on the side; cut the loaf lengthwise before slicing across. Prefer individual mini meatloaves? The next recipe gives directions for freezing and reheating mini meatloaves.

2 cups water
2 (6 ounce) packages Stove Top stuffing mix or dry bread cubes
3 pounds ground beef
2 teaspoons garlic powder
1/2 teaspoon chili powder
1 cup barbecue sauce
1 cup shredded cheddar cheese
Preheat oven to 350°F.

In a large bowl, combine water and stuffing mix to partially rehydrate. Add ground beef, garlic powder, and chili powder; mix until well combined.

Transfer to a large loaf pan or 2 smaller ones. Make a depression in the center of the meatloaf with the back of a spoon. Spoon the barbecue sauce into the depression and around the rest of the top of the meatloaf.

Bake for 35 to 45 minutes, or until cooked through; temperature on an instant-read thermometer should be

160°F. Sprinkle cheddar cheese on top, and bake for 5 to 10 more minutes until cheese melts. Remove pan(s) from oven; let stand for 10 minutes. Remove the meatloaf from the loaf pan(s), and cool completely.

To Freeze: Transfer to a freezer-safe bag, or wrap in plastic wrap and foil. Label with name and date. Freeze up to 1 month.

To Serve: Thaw in refrigerator for 8 to 9 hours before serving. Preheat oven to 250°F. Wrap entire meatloaf completely in foil, and place on a baking sheet. Cook for 20 minutes. Cut into slices.

Italian Mini Meatloaf Muffins

Makes: 24

Make-Ahead: Freeze up to 1 month

A roast meat of some type or a ham is typically the star of the holiday meal. These little meatloaves aren't meant to be the main player, but with the optional colorful serving sauces, they will add variety to the mix of dishes for the meal.

2 cups water

2 (6 ounce) packages Stove Top stuffing mix or dry bread cubes

3 pounds ground beef

2 teaspoons garlic powder

2 teaspoons Italian seasoning

1 cup pasta sauce

1 cup shredded mozzarella cheese

TO SERVE

1/2 cup prepared pesto (optional)

1/2 cup pasta sauce (optional)

Preheat oven to 350°F. Grease two 12-cup muffin tins.

In a large bowl, combine water and stuffing mix to partially rehydrate. Add ground beef, garlic powder, and Italian seasoning; mix until well combined.

Spoon meat mixture into muffin cups. Make a depression in the center of each meat muffin with the back of a spoon. Spoon the pasta sauce into the depression, and drizzle a little sauce on the rest of the muffin.

Bake for 30 minutes, or until cooked through; temperature on an instant-read thermometer should be 160°F. Sprinkle mozzarella cheese on top, and bake for 5 to 10 more minutes until cheese melts. Remove tins from oven; let stand for 10 minutes. Remove the meatloaf muffins from the muffin cups to a cookie sheet, and cool completely.

To Freeze: Freeze for 4 to 5 hours. Transfer to freezer-safe bags. Label with name and date. Freeze up to 1 month.

To Serve: Thaw in refrigerator for 8 to 9 hours before serving. Preheat oven to 250°F. Place meatloaf muffins back in muffin tins. Wrap tins in foil, leaving a little space above the tops of meatloaves but securing the foil on all edges of the tins. Bake for 15 minutes. Remove foil, and arrange muffins on serving platter. Top each with a decorative drizzle of pesto and/or pasta sauce, if desired.

Refrigerator Recipes

Pickled Peaches

Adapted from a recipe by Jeanne Cleary, Wichita (2nd Place Winner in Category), as published in The Wichita Eagle 1999 Holiday Cookbook supplement

Makes 2 quarts

Make-Ahead: Refrigerate up to 3 weeks

This is one of the sides that I made for my first Thanksgiving. My then-husband did not like cranberries, and I wanted to make a special "fruity" side for him. I found this recipe in a newspaper's online holiday cookbook. It was a big hit! When I took it to a larger family Thanksgiving dinner, everyone loved it. I've made it every Thanksgiving since. I prefer to use peach slices so the pickling liquid really soaks in; I never use whole spices, just the ground ones. I prefer balsamic vinegar to the original white vinegar called for, as it gives a more subtle, sophisticated flavor. I will quite often make 1 1/2 times the recipe as it is popular with all my family. The pickling liquid is fantastic on vanilla ice cream or crumbled pumpkin bread.

2 (29 ounce) cans peach halves or slices in heavy syrup (see TIP)

1 cup white sugar

1/2 cup white or balsamic vinegar

3 cinnamon sticks (2 teaspoons cinnamon may be substituted)

Whole cloves (approximately half of a 0.6 ounce jar) (or a dash ground cloves)

Drain peaches and set aside, reserving liquid. Pour peach syrup into a 2-quart saucepan. Add sugar, vinegar, cinnamon, and ground cloves, if using, to peach juice. Heat to boiling; continue cooking for 10 minutes, stirring frequently with a whisk. Place drained peach halves cut side down in a glass 13" x 9" baking dish. (See TIP.) Place 2 to 3 whole cloves into each peach half if not using ground cloves. Pour hot peach juice over the peach halves. Cool, cover with clear plastic wrap, and refrigerate overnight. Remove cloves before eating.

TIPS

- You need to buy the version in heavy syrup, as it is an essential component of the pickling liquid.
- Since I don't use whole cloves, I usually just add the peaches into the pickling liquid in the pot after it has boiled, taking the pot off the heat. When cool, I divide peaches and liquid into quart-sized storage containers.

Smoky Cheddar Steak Fries From Scratch

Serves: 8

Make-Ahead: Refrigerate up to 3 days

2 pounds red or Yukon gold potatoes, scrubbed and cut lengthwise into 3/4" wedges

2 tablespoons extra virgin olive oil

1 tablespoon smoked paprika

1 teaspoon garlic powder

1 teaspoon ground cumin

TO SERVE

Salt, to taste

2/3 cup red bell pepper, finely chopped

2 ounces sharp cheddar cheese, finely shredded (reduced fat OK)

1/4 cup finely chopped fresh cilantro

Preheat oven to 425° F.

Line one large or 2 medium baking sheets with foil. Place potatoes in a large bowl, and toss with oil.

Combine paprika, garlic powder, and cumin in a small bowl. Sprinkle spice mixture over the potatoes. Stir the potatoes to coat evenly.

Spread the potatoes on the baking sheet(s) in a single layer. Bake in batches if using 2 baking sheets.

Bake for about 20 minutes, or until light golden brown on top and tender inside. Turn the potatoes halfway through baking. When done, remove from the oven, and allow to cool completely.

To Refrigerate: Transfer to an airtight container or food storage bag. Label with name, if desired. Refrigerate up to 3 days.

To Serve

Place potatoes on a baking sheet. Broil for a few minutes until crisp; watch so they do not burn. Turn the potatoes to crisp the other side.

Mix salt, bell pepper, and cheese in a bowl. Sprinkle over the potatoes.

Broil until the cheese melts.

Garnish with cilantro.

Loaded Mashed Potato Casserole

Serves: 10 to 14

Make-Ahead: Refrigerate up to 2 days

4 1/2 pounds russet potatoes, peeled and cubed

12 ounces sour cream or plain Greek yogurt

1 1/2 cups whole or 2% milk, plus extra if needed

12 ounces sharp cheddar cheese, grated

3/4 cup grated Parmesan cheese

1 teaspoon kosher salt

Freshly ground pepper, to taste

3 medium shallots, minced

TOPPING

6 slices good quality bacon, cooked and crumbled

1/3 cup thinly sliced green onions

1/2 cup grated Cheddar cheese

In a large pot of salted water, bring the potatoes to a boil over medium-high heat. Gently boil the potatoes until they are cooked through, about 10 minutes. Turn off heat.

Drain the potatoes thoroughly, and return them to the pot. Add sour cream and milk to the potatoes, and mash with a potato masher until the desired consistency is achieved. Add more milk if needed. Stir in cheddar cheese, Parmesan cheese, salt, pepper, and shallots; mix until well incorporated.

Spread mixture evenly in a 13" x 9" baking dish. Sprinkle bacon, green onion, and cheddar cheese on top.

To Refrigerate: Cover the dish with foil, and place in the refrigerator up to 2 days. Label with name, if desired.

To Serve: Remove from the refrigerator a half hour before baking. Bake, still covered in foil, at 350°F for 30 to 40 minutes. Remove foil, and bake for 10 more minutes.

Leftovers can be stored for 3 to 4 days in the refrigerator.

Pecan Brown Bread Stuffing With Apples And Cherries

Serves: 10

Make-Ahead: Refrigerate up to 2 days

1 (1.5- to 2-pound) loaf whole wheat bread, cut into cubes

1/4 cup butter, divided use, plus extra to grease baking dish

4 cloves garlic, thinly sliced

2 medium onion, chopped

2 celery stalks, chopped

Salt, to taste

Freshly ground pepper, to taste

1 tablespoon minced fresh sage

1 tablespoon minced fresh thyme

3/4 cup roughly chopped dried apples

2/3 cup dried cherries

2/3 cup pecans, chopped

1/2 cup unfiltered apple juice

1 cup vegetable broth

Place bread cubes in a large bowl.

Melt 1 tablespoon butter in a skillet over medium heat. Add garlic, onion, celery, salt, and pepper; sauté until onions are translucent. Stir in sage and thyme, and sauté for 10 seconds, or until aromatic. Turn off heat. Add apples, cherries, and pecans. Mix well, and add to bowl of bread. Toss well.

Melt remaining butter in a skillet over medium heat. Add apple juice and broth. When liquid begins to lightly bubble, pour it over the bread. Toss until bread is well coated with the liquid.

To Refrigerate: Transfer to a 13" x 9" baking dish lightly greased with butter, and tightly cover with foil. Alternatively, stuffing can be stored in gallon-sized food storage bags. Place in the refrigerator for 2 to 3 days. Label with name, if desired.

To Serve: Remove from the refrigerator, and let stand at room temperature for 30 minutes. Uncover, and bake at 350°F for 35 to 45 minutes, or until the top is golden brown.

Oyster And Wild Rice Casserole

Serves: 6

Make-Ahead: Refrigerate up to 3 days

1 (4.5 ounce) package long grain and wild rice mix (like Mahatma)

3/4 cup plus 2 tablespoons beef broth, divided use

1 1/2 tablespoons butter, divided use

Hot sauce, to taste

1 quart shucked oysters, drained well

1/4 teaspoon fine sea salt

Freshly ground pepper, to taste

Cooking spray

1 shallot, minced

1 clove garlic, minced

1/2 can (from a 10.75 ounces can) cream of mushroom soup

1/4 cup half-and-half

TO SERVE

Chopped fresh parsley, to garnish (optional)

Crushed red pepper, to taste

Prepare rice mix according to package directions, substituting 3/4 cup broth for part of the liquid. Remove from heat, and let stand for 5 minutes. Drain, and add 1 tablespoon butter and hot sauce to taste. Fluff with a fork, and mix to distribute evenly.

Melt remaining butter in a skillet over medium heat. Add oysters, and cook until edges are curled. Discard the pan juices, and set oysters aside.

Grease an 11" x 7" baking dish with cooking spray. Spread half the rice mixture evenly over the bottom of the dish. Distribute oysters over the rice. Season with salt and pepper. Spread the remaining rice mixture over the oysters. Set aside.

Spray a saucepan with cooking spray, and place it over medium heat. Add shallots and garlic; sauté for 1 minute. Add mushroom soup and remaining broth. Heat through. Remove from heat, and add half-and-half; whisk until well combined. Pour evenly over the rice mixture in the baking dish.

To Refrigerate: Cover the dish with plastic wrap first and then with foil. Label with name, if desired. Refrigerate up to 3 days.

To Serve

Remove baking dish from refrigerator, and let stand at room temperature for 30 minutes. Remove foil and plastic wrap. Bake at 350°F for 30 to 40 minutes, or until the top is golden brown.

Sprinkle parsley (if using) and crushed red pepper on top.

Squash Gratin With Poblanos & Cream

Serves: 6

Make-Ahead: Refrigerate up to 2 days

3 large poblanos (about 3/4 pound)

1/4 cup plus 1/2 tablespoon extra virgin olive oil, divided use

1 large butternut squash (2 pounds), peeled, halved, deseeded, and cut into 1/2" slices

Salt, to taste

Freshly ground pepper, to taste

3/4 teaspoon chopped fresh thyme, divided use

1 medium onion, thinly sliced

1/2 teaspoon chopped oregano

2 large cloves garlic, thinly sliced

1/4 cup heavy cream

6 tablespoons crème fraîche or sour cream

4 ounces Monterey Jack cheese, shredded

4 ounces farmer cheese

TO SERVE

Toasted pumpkin seeds

Place poblanos on gas burners directly over the flame until charred. Turn a couple of times while roasting for even charring. If you don't have a gas stove—or don't feel comfortable roasting chiles directly on the stovetop—you can also broil them. Just be sure to watch closely, and turn so they char evenly all over.

Preheat oven to 400°F.

Remove chiles, and place in a bowl. Cover the bowl with plastic wrap, and let peppers cool completely. Peel the peppers, and slice into thin strips.

Brush 3 tablespoons oil on the butternut squash slices, and arrange on a rimmed baking sheet in a single layer. Use 2 sheets if needed. Sprinkle salt, pepper, and 1/2 teaspoon thyme over the slices. Bake for about 25 to 30 minutes, or until tender.

Heat remaining oil in a deep skillet over medium heat. When oil is heated, add onion, oregano, garlic, and 1/4 teaspoon thyme; sauté until onions turn translucent. Stir in poblano strips, and cook for 3 to 4 minutes. Stir in cream, and cook until thick.

Remove from heat. Add crème fraîche and more salt and pepper if desired; mix well.

Pour half the poblano mixture into a 13" x 9" baking dish. Place half the butternut squash slices over the poblano layer. Next layer with half of the Monterey cheese followed by half of the farmer cheese. Repeat these layers once more.

To Refrigerate: Cover the dish with plastic wrap, and refrigerate up to 2 days. Label with name, if desired.

To Serve: Remove dish from the refrigerator, and let stand at room temperature for an hour. Bake uncovered at 350°F for 30 minutes, or until golden brown on top. Remove from the oven, and let stand for 10 minutes. Sprinkle pumpkin seeds on top.

Smoky Creamed Kale

Serves: 12

Make-Ahead: Refrigerate up to 2 days

2 (1 pound) bags chopped kale (or 3 pounds fresh kale, hard ribs and stems discarded and leaves chopped)

1 cup butter

1 small white onion, finely chopped

12 cloves garlic, minced

1/2 cup all-purpose flour

4 cups whole milk

2/3 cup finely grated Parmesan cheese

2 teaspoons smoked paprika

1 teaspoon dry mustard

Freshly ground pepper, to taste

2 teaspoons salt, or to taste

Bring a large pot of salted water to a boil over high heat. While pot comes up to a boil, fill a large bowl with tap water and 12 or so ice cubes.

When water boils, add kale, and cook for 1 minute. Drain into a colander, and immediately submerge in the large bowl of ice water. Stir the kale to cool completely. Drain water, and pat leaves dry with a clean kitchen towel or paper towels.

Melt butter in a deep skillet over medium-high heat. When butter is melted, add onion and garlic; sauté until the onions are translucent. Sprinkle flour over onions. Lower heat to medium, and stir constantly for 3 minutes. Do not brown the flour. Add milk, whisking constantly until the sauce thickens. Bring to a low boil, and hold for 5 minutes. Lower heat, and simmer for 2 to 3 minutes, whisking occasionally. Add cheese, paprika, mustard, pepper, and salt; mix well. Add kale, and stir to coat. Heat for 2 to 3 minutes (until kale wilts slightly). Turn off the heat. Transfer into a 13" x 9" dish. Let cool completely.

To Refrigerate: Cover tightly with plastic wrap; it should touch the kale. Refrigerate up to 2 days.

To Serve: Remove from refrigerator, and let stand at room temperature for 30 minutes. Discard plastic wrap. Bake uncovered for 30 minutes at 375°F, or until bubbling and heated through. Remove from oven, and let stand for 5 minutes.

Mixed Green Salad With Grapefruit & Cranberries

Serves: 12

Make-Ahead: Refrigerate components separately up to 2 days

Store components (grapefruit, dressing, salad) of this recipe separately up to 2 days. This is a great take-along, as the salad components and grapefruit can be tossed early in the day and will travel well in a large covered bowl. Just be sure to bring the dressing!

The dressing would keep for weeks without the green onions.

I think this is a great technique for making salads for any get-together. A standard vinaigrette (with no vegetables) can be make weeks in advance. Salad greens can be prepared 3 days in advance. Other fruits and vegetables can be prepped in advance, too, though times will vary. Keep components that have different shelf lives stored in separate containers.

2 red grapefruits

DRESSING

1/4 cup extra virgin olive oil

1 tablespoon white wine vinegar

1/4 cup finely sliced green onions

Freshly ground pepper, to taste

Salt, to taste

SALAD

1/3 cup pine nuts

8 cups butter lettuce, torn

1 (14 ounce) can hearts of palm, drained and chopped into bite-sized pieces

6 cups baby spinach

1/3 cup dried cranberries

Peel grapefruits. Separate into segments, removing membrane around each segment; reserve membranes. Discard seeds. Cut each segment into 2 pieces. Transfer grapefruit into an airtight container. Squeeze membranes directly over the grapefruit, catching the juice in the container. Store in the refrigerator up to 2 days.

DRESSING: Add olive oil, vinegar, green onions, pepper, and salt into a small jar. Tighten the lid, and shake vigorously until well combined. Place dressing in refrigerator up to 2 days.

Toast the pine nuts for a few minutes in a small pan over medium-low heat until aromatic and light brown. Turn off heat, and let cool completely. Transfer to an airtight container.

To Serve

Transfer grapefruit segments into a serving bowl. Add lettuce, hearts of palm, and spinach; toss well. Refrigerate for 3 to 4 hours.

Pour dressing on top just before serving; toss well. Add cranberries and pine nuts.

Part 2

Crockpot Mushrooms

"Excellent mushrooms to serve with steak or just as a side."

Serving: 4 | Prep: 5 m | Cook: 3 h | Ready in: 3 h 5 m

Ingredients

- 1 pound mushrooms
- 1/2 cup butter
- 1 (1 ounce) envelope ranch salad dressing mix

Direction

- Put mushrooms, butter, and ranch salad dressing mix in a slow cooker.
- Cook on Low for 3-4 hours.

Nutrition Information

- Calories: 246 calories
- Total Fat: 23.4 g
- Cholesterol: 61 mg
- Sodium: 659 mg
- Total Carbohydrate: 7.2 g
- Protein: 3.7 g

Crusty Herb Potato Wedges

"Simple and delicious. The key is tossing the spices with the potatoes and oil in a bowl and then on to the pan. The silicone mat we are baking on is a very nice thing to have in your kitchen."

Serving: 2 | Prep: 10 m | Cook: 35 m | Ready in: 45 m

Ingredients

- 2 Russet potatoes, each cut into 6 equal wedges
- olive oil
- 1 tablespoon herbes de Provence
- 1 pinch paprika, or to taste
- salt and ground black pepper to taste

Direction

- Preheat oven to 425 degrees F (220 degrees C). Line a baking sheet with a silicone baking mat.
- Toss potato wedges, olive oil, herbes de Provence, paprika, salt, and black pepper together in a bowl until potatoes are evenly coated. Place wedges on their sides onto the prepared baking sheet.
- Bake in the preheated oven for 15 minutes. Flip potatoes onto their other sides; return to oven and cook until crusty and golden brown, about 20 minutes more.

Nutrition Information

- Calories: 225 calories
- Total Fat: 7 g
- Cholesterol: 0 mg
- Sodium: 13 mg
- Total Carbohydrate: 37.5 g
- Protein: 4.4 g

Delicious Homemade Orange Zest Kale

"This is one of my favorite recipes that my BFF and I made up, and it ended up tasting amazing! This recipe is great for vegetarians, vegans, and healthy eaters, so enjoy!"

Serving: 2 | Prep: 5 m | Cook: 5 m | Ready in: 10 m
Ingredients

- 1 tablespoon olive oil

- 5 ounces baby kale (such as Olivia's®)
- 2 tablespoons grated orange zest
- 2 tablespoons orange juice
- salt and ground black pepper to taste

Direction

- Heat a skillet over high heat. Drizzle olive oil into the skillet. Add half the kale to the skillet; sauté until mostly wilted, about 2 minutes. Add remaining kale to the skillet; sauté until wilted, about 2 minutes. Stir in orange zest and juice. Season with salt and pepper.

Nutrition Information
- Calories: 108 calories
- Total Fat: 7.3 g
- Cholesterol: 0 mg
- Sodium: 108 mg
- Total Carbohydrate: 10.2 g
- Protein: 2.5 g

Divine French Fries

"Delicious and easy recipe for a side dish or appetizer."

Serving: 4 | Prep: 15 m | Cook: 30 m | Ready in: 50 m
Ingredients

- cooking spray
- 1 pound potatoes, cut into strips - or more to taste
- salt and ground black pepper to taste
- 1 tablespoon white truffle oil, or to taste
- 2 teaspoons chopped fresh parsley, or more to taste

Direction

- Preheat oven to 350 degrees F (175 degrees C). Spray a baking sheet with cooking spray.

- Spread potato strips evenly onto the prepared baking sheet. Spray potatoes with cooking spray; season with salt and pepper.
- Bake in the preheated oven until potatoes are tender, 30 to 40 minutes. Cool for 5 minutes.
- Transfer fries to a large bowl. Add truffle oil, parsley, and salt to fries; toss to coat.

Nutrition Information

- Calories: 120 calories
- Total Fat: 3.7 g
- Cholesterol: 0 mg
- Sodium: 7 mg
- Total Carbohydrate: 19.9 g
- Protein: 2.3 g

Down South Pinto Beans

"My grandmother always brought these wonderful pinto beans with pork jowl to the table at mealtimes, along with cornbread and onions. Yummy. A true Southern tradition."

Serving: 8 | Prep: 5 m | Cook: 3 h 5 m | Ready in: 3 h 10 m
Ingredients
- 2 cups dried pinto beans
- 4 quarts water, or more as needed
- 4 (1 ounce) slices pork jowl, or more to taste
- 2 tablespoons white sugar
- salt and ground black pepper to taste

Direction

- Wash pinto beans thoroughly and place in a large stockpot. Add 4 quarts water, pork jowl, sugar, salt, and pepper. Bring to a rolling boil over high heat. Reduce heat to a simmer; cook until beans are tender and tasty, 3 to 4 hours. Add water throughout cooking as needed; do not let the beans cook dry.

Nutrition Information
- Calories: 272 calories
- Total Fat: 10.5 g
- Cholesterol: 13 mg
- Sodium: 43 mg
- Total Carbohydrate: 33.3 g
- Protein: 11.2 g

Easiest Asparagus Recipe

"I have always been good at sauteeing asparagus, but this is one of my favorite methods to create a sweet and traditional appetizer."

Serving: 5 | Prep: 5 m | Cook: 10 m | Ready in: 15 m
Ingredients
- 2 tablespoons butter, or more as needed
- 1 bunch asparagus, trimmed
- 1 teaspoon honey
- 1/8 teaspoon garlic powder
- 1/8 teaspoon cayenne pepper

Direction
- Melt 2 tablespoons butter in a skillet over medium-low heat. Cook asparagus in melted butter, stirring a few times, until tender, 6 to 8 minutes.
- Drizzle honey over the asparagus and stir to coat; season with garlic powder and cayenne pepper.

Nutrition Information

- Calories: 64 calories
- Total Fat: 4.7 g
- Cholesterol: 12 mg
- Sodium: 35 mg
- Total Carbohydrate: 4.8 g
- Protein: 2.1 g

Easiest Corn On The Cob

"This proves something that I've known for years: no matter how great a kitchen technique is, unless you use it regularly, you'll forget about it. This technique for making corn on the cob works perfectly, and I hope you give it a try soon."

Serving: 1 | Prep: 5 m | Cook: 5 m | Ready in: 10 m

Ingredients
- 1 ear fresh corn in the husk
- 1 teaspoon butter, or more to taste
- salt to taste

Direction
- Heat corn in the microwave until cooked through and tender, about 3 1/2 minutes.
- Hold the tapered end of the corn with a towel over a cutting board. Cut the bottom 1-inch off of the thick end of the cob. Squeeze tapered end of corn cob out of husk and silk.
- Spread butter over corn and season with salt.

Nutrition Information
- Calories: 113 calories
- Total Fat: 5.1 g
- Cholesterol: 11 mg
- Sodium: 42 mg
- Total Carbohydrate: 17.1 g
- Protein: 2.9 g

Easy Cheesy Potatoes

"Great easy recipe."

Serving: 8 | Prep: 5 m | Cook: 1 h 20 m | Ready in: 1 h 35 m

Ingredients

- 2 (10.75 ounce) cans cream of chicken soup
- 1 (8 ounce) package cream cheese
- 3/4 cup milk
- 2 pounds hash brown potatoes
- 2 cups shredded Cheddar cheese

Direction

- Preheat oven to 350 degrees F (175 degrees C).
- Stir cream of chicken soup, cream cheese, and milk together in a saucepan over medium heat and cook until the cheese is completely melted and the liquid is heated through, about 5 minutes.
- Spread hash brown potatoes into a casserole dish; pour soup mixture over the potatoes.
- Bake in preheated oven until the edges begin to brown, about 1 hour and 15 minutes.
- Sprinkle Cheddar cheese over the dish; let the cheese melt as the dish cools slightly before serving, about 10 minutes.

Nutrition Information

- Calories: 387 calories
- Total Fat: 31.3 g
- Cholesterol: 66 mg
- Sodium: 821 mg
- Total Carbohydrate: 28.5 g
- Protein: 13.4 g

Easy Chinese Broccoli

"Chinese broccoli is also known as jiè-lán or gai lan. It pairs well with most Chinese dishes."

Serving: 2 | Prep: 5 m | Cook: 10 m | Ready in: 15 m

Ingredients
- 1 pound Chinese broccoli
- 3 tablespoons oyster sauce
- 1 teaspoon brown sugar
- 1/2 teaspoon sesame oil (optional)

Direction
- Pour about 1 inch of water into a saucepan and bring to a boil. Place Chinese broccoli in the saucepan and cover with the lid. Cook until stems are tender, 2 to 5 minutes. Use tongs to transfer to a plate.
- Mix oyster sauce, brown sugar, and sesame oil together in a bowl. Drizzle sauce over the cooked Chinese broccoli.

Nutrition Information
- Calories: 116 calories
- Total Fat: 2.5 g
- Cholesterol: 0 mg
- Sodium: 325 mg
- Total Carbohydrate: 21.6 g
- Protein: 5.4 g

Easy Fried Zucchini

"These are delicious, easy, and can be made from ingredients you already have in the kitchen. They are always a big hit in our home."

Serving: 4 | Prep: 10 m | Cook: 10 m | Ready in: 20 m

Ingredients

- 2 zucchinis, cut into 1/2-inch slices
- 2 eggs, beaten
- 1 sleeve buttery round crackers (such as Ritz®), crushed
- 2 tablespoons olive oil
- salt and ground black pepper to taste

Direction

- Coat each zucchini slice with egg, then press into cracker crumbs, coating both sides. Shake off excess and place the breaded zucchini onto a plate while breading the rest; do not stack.
- Heat olive oil in a large skillet over medium heat. Pan fry zucchini until crust browns and zucchini softens, about 3 minutes on each side. Season with salt and pepper.

Nutrition Information

- Calories: 256 calories
- Total Fat: 17.3 g
- Cholesterol: 93 mg
- Sodium: 301 mg
- Total Carbohydrate: 20 g
- Protein: 6 g

Easy Garlic Green Beans

"This very simple quick and easy side dish is very popular in my family."

Serving: 4 | Prep: 5 m | Cook: 15 m | Ready in: 20 m

Ingredients

- 1 tablespoon butter
- 1 pound frozen whole green beans
- 1 large clove garlic, crushed

- 1/2 teaspoon coarse salt

Direction

- Melt butter in a skillet over medium heat; cook and stir green beans and garlic until beans begin to thaw. Season with salt and continue cooking and stirring until beans are lightly browned, 10 to 15 minutes.

Nutrition Information

- Calories: 64 calories
- Total Fat: 2.9 g
- Cholesterol: 8 mg
- Sodium: 261 mg
- Total Carbohydrate: 7.7 g
- Protein: 1.6 g

Easy German Red Cabbage

"Easy and inexpensive side dish that is excellent with Round Steak Sauerbraten from this site."

Serving: 12 | Prep: 5 m | Cook: 20 m | Ready in: 25 m

Ingredients

- 2 (16 ounce) packages fresh sauerkraut, drained
- 1 (16 ounce) jar pickled beets, undrained
- 2 tablespoons butter
- 2 bay leaves
- salt and ground black pepper to taste

Direction

- Heat sauerkraut, beets and beet juice, butter, and bay leaves in a large pot over medium heat; season with salt and pepper. Simmer until heated through, about 15 minutes.

Nutrition Information

- Calories: 56 calories
- Total Fat: 2.1 g
- Cholesterol: 5 mg
- Sodium: 614 mg
- Total Carbohydrate: 9.4 g
- Protein: 1 g

Easy Glazed Carrots

"These glazed carrots are easy and simple to make. They make a great kid's snack or even a side dish to go with a meal."

Serving: 4 | Prep: 5 m | Cook: 5 m | Ready in: 10 m

Ingredients
- 1 (16 ounce) can sliced carrots, drained
- 2/3 cup brown sugar
- 1/4 cup butter
- 2 tablespoons orange marmalade

Direction
- Place carrots into a microwave-safe bowl; add brown sugar, butter, and orange marmalade to carrots. Cover bowl loosely with plastic wrap and cook in microwave on high power for 3 minutes; stir. If butter and marmalade aren't completely melted, continue cooking on high power for 30-second intervals, stirring after each interval, until carrots are coated with glaze.

Nutrition Information
- Calories: 244 calories
- Total Fat: 11.7 g
- Cholesterol: 31 mg
- Sodium: 363 mg
- Total Carbohydrate: 36.4 g

- Protein: 0.8 g

Easy Italian Grilled Zucchini

"This recipe is super-easy to make and is very delicious, considering how easy it is to prepare!"

Serving: 6 | Prep: 5 m | Cook: 15 m | Ready in: 50 m

Ingredients
- 1 (8 ounce) bottle Italian-style salad dressing
- 2 zucchinis, cut into thick rounds
- salt and ground black pepper to taste

Direction
- Pour Italian-style salad dressing into a resealable plastic bag. Add the zucchini and coat with the dressing. Season generously with salt and black pepper. Squeeze excess air from the bag and seal. Marinate in the refrigerator 30 to 60 minutes.
- Preheat an outdoor grill for medium-high heat and lightly oil the grate.
- Remove zucchini from bag; discard dressing.
- Cook zucchini rounds on preheated grill until lightly browned and soft in the center, 7 to 10 minutes per side.

Nutrition Information
- Calories: 114 calories
- Total Fat: 10.5 g
- Cholesterol: 0 mg
- Sodium: 614 mg
- Total Carbohydrate: 5.2 g
- Protein: 0.6 g

Easy Lime Shredded Brussels Sprouts

"This is a super easy side dish. For those of you scared of Brussels sprouts, please give these a try as they have made people who think they don't like them into fans!"

Serving: 4 | Prep: 10 m | Cook: 6 m | Ready in: 16 m

Ingredients
- 1/4 cup butter
- 1 pound Brussels sprouts, halved and shredded
- 1 lime, juiced, or more to taste
- 1 pinch kosher salt and ground black pepper to taste

Direction
- Heat butter in a skillet over medium heat. Cook and stir Brussels sprouts in the melted butter until tender, 6 to 8 minutes. Squeeze lime juice over sprouts and season with kosher salt and pepper.

Nutrition Information
- Calories: 151 calories
- Total Fat: 11.9 g
- Cholesterol: 31 mg
- Sodium: 210 mg
- Total Carbohydrate: 10.5 g
- Protein: 4 g

Easy Marinated Brussels Sprouts

"Very simple but delicious way to serve Brussels sprouts. If you have time, you may want to make your own Italian dressing; if not, the bottled kind works just fine. We like them as a side dish or even mixed into a tossed salad."

Serving: 6 | Prep: 10 m | Cook: 15 m | Ready in: 4 h 25 m

Ingredients

- 1 pound Brussels sprouts, trimmed
- 1 (16 ounce) bottle zesty Italian-style salad dressing
- 3 dashes hot sauce, or to taste (optional)

Direction

- Bring a large pot of lightly salted water to a boil. Cook Brussels sprouts in the boiling water, stirring occasionally until tender, about 15 minutes. Drain and transfer to a large bowl.
- Pour Italian dressing and hot sauce over Brussels sprouts; toss to coat. Marinate in the refrigerator, stirring occasionally, for 4 hours.

Nutrition Information

- Calories: 247 calories
- Total Fat: 21.1 g
- Cholesterol: 0 mg
- Sodium: 1252 mg
- Total Carbohydrate: 14.5 g
- Protein: 2.8 g

Easy Masala Hash Browns

"Hash browns that everyone will want seconds of! My family loves these. And my brother brings over his kids as well every second week to enjoy these as well."

Serving: 8 | Prep: 10 m | Cook: 12 m | Ready in: 22 m

Ingredients

- 4 potatoes, peeled and cut into 2-inch pieces
- 1/2 cup canola oil
- 2 teaspoons garam masala
- 1/2 teaspoon seasoned salt

Direction

- Set oven rack about 6 inches from the heat source and preheat the oven's broiler.
- Combine oil, garam masala, and seasoned salt together in a large bowl. Add potato pieces and toss to coat. Spread on an ungreased baking sheet.
- Broil potatoes in the preheated oven until starting to brown, about 7 minutes. Remove from oven and flip potatoes over. Return to the oven and continue broiling until golden brown, about 5 minutes more.

Nutrition Information

- Calories: 208 calories
- Total Fat: 14.2 g
- Cholesterol: 0 mg
- Sodium: 65 mg
- Total Carbohydrate: 19 g
- Protein: 2.2 g

Easy Pineapple Bake

"We first had this at a special Easter dinner served for our family at the Ronald McDonald House in Philadelphia. It was a side dish served with ham, but could also be served as a dessert. I wish I could give credit to the sweet lady who shared the recipe with me."

Serving: 8 | Prep: 15 m | Cook: 45 m | Ready in: 1 h
Ingredients

- 3/4 cup white sugar
- 1/2 cup butter, softened
- 4 eggs
- 5 slices day-old bread, cut into cubes
- 1 (20 ounce) can crushed pineapple, drained

Direction
- Preheat oven to 350 degrees F (175 degrees C).
- Beat sugar and butter together in a bowl using an electric mixer until smooth and creamy. Add eggs and beat until smooth. Stir bread and pineapple into creamed butter mixture; pour into a 1-quart baking dish.
- Bake in the preheated oven until lightly browned and eggs are set, 45 to 50 minutes.

Nutrition Information
- Calories: 294 calories
- Total Fat: 14.6 g
- Cholesterol: 124 mg
- Sodium: 224 mg
- Total Carbohydrate: 37.8 g
- Protein: 4.8 g

Easy Polish Noodles

"Growing up in South Bend, Indiana, Polish dinner buffets are extremely common at weddings and funerals. Polish noodles are a staple at these events and served alongside Polish sausage, green beans, mashed potatoes and chicken gravy, and fried chicken. While at a Polish meat market, an elderly Polish lady passed this recipe on to me upon request."

Serving: 6 | Prep: 5 m | Cook: 35 m | Ready in: 40 m
Ingredients

- 1 (49.5 fluid ounce) can chicken broth
- 1/2 cup water, or as desired
- 1 tablespoon chicken soup base, or more to taste
- 1 (16 ounce) package kluski noodles

Direction
- Combine chicken broth, water, and chicken base in a 6-quart saucepan and bring to a boil. Add kluski noodles, reduce heat, and simmer until liquid is completely absorbed, 30 to 40 minutes.

Nutrition Information
- Calories: 310 calories
- Total Fat: 4.1 g
- Cholesterol: 69 mg
- Sodium: 1515 mg
- Total Carbohydrate: 54.8 g
- Protein: 12.1 g

Easy Potato Dumplings

"A must to go with Polish sausage and sauerkraut! I didn't want to dig for my paper copy of the recipe, so I thought I'd search for it and I was shocked it wasn't on here."

Serving: 12 | Prep: 20 m | Cook: 15 m | Ready in: 35 m

Ingredients
- 6 cups leftover mashed potatoes
- 4 cups all-purpose flour
- 3/4 cup dry farina cereal (such as Cream of Wheat®)
- 3 eggs
- 3 egg yolks
- 2 teaspoons salt

Direction

- Mix potatoes, flour, cereal, eggs, egg yolks, and salt together in a bowl using your hands until the mixture comes together into a workable dough. Roll dough into 4- to 5-inch long logs with the diameter of a quarter.
- Bring a large pot of water to a boil, add the dough logs, and cook until the dumplings float, about 15 minutes.

Nutrition Information

- Calories: 310 calories
- Total Fat: 3.4 g
- Cholesterol: 100 mg
- Sodium: 725 mg
- Total Carbohydrate: 59 g
- Protein: 9.7 g

Easy Pressure Cooker Potatoes

"This is the easiest way I have come up with for cooking whole, skin-on potatoes to perfection for use in whatever recipe you need them for."

Serving: 8 | Prep: 5 m | Cook: 15 m | Ready in: 20 m
Ingredients

- 2 cups water
- 8 russet potatoes, scrubbed

Direction

- Pour water into the bottom of a pressure cooker (such as Presto(R)). Place a trivet into the pressure cooker and turn the heat on high.
- Place potatoes in a single layer in the pressure cooker and lock the lid. Cook over high heat until the pressure

regulator reaches 15 psi, 5 to 10 minutes. Remove from heat. Allow pressure to drop naturally, 10 minutes. Unlock and remove lid.

Nutrition Information
- Calories: 224 calories
- Total Fat: 0.2 g
- Cholesterol: 0 mg
- Sodium: 16 mg
- Total Carbohydrate: 51.2 g
- Protein: 6.1 g

Easy Roasted Broccoli

"Easy roasted broccoli. My favorite part is the roasted sliced stem pieces."

Serving: 4 | Prep: 10 m | Cook: 20 m | Ready in: 30 m

Ingredients
- 14 ounces broccoli
- 1 tablespoon olive oil
- salt and ground black pepper to taste

Direction
- Preheat oven to 400 degrees F (200 degrees C).
- Cut broccoli florets from the stalk. Peel the stalk and slice into 1/4-inch slices. Mix florets and stem pieces with olive oil in a bowl and transfer to a baking sheet; season with salt and pepper.
- Roast in the preheated oven until broccoli is tender and lightly browned, about 18 minutes.

Nutrition Information
- Calories: 63 calories
- Total Fat: 3.7 g

- Cholesterol: 0 mg
- Sodium: 71 mg
- Total Carbohydrate: 6.5 g
- Protein: 2.8 g

Easy Roasted Cabbage

"Delicious and healthy roasted cabbage slices are sure to please."

Serving: 6 | Prep: 10 m | Cook: 40 m | Ready in: 50 m

Ingredients
- 1 head cabbage, sliced into six 1-inch pieces
- 6 tablespoons olive oil
- salt and ground black pepper to taste

Direction
- Preheat oven to 425 degrees F (220 degrees C).
- Brush each cabbage piece on both sides with olive oil and season with salt and black pepper. Arrange in a single layer on a baking sheet.
- Bake in the preheated oven until tender, 40 to 55 minutes.

Nutrition Information
- Calories: 169 calories
- Total Fat: 13.7 g
- Cholesterol: 0 mg
- Sodium: 62 mg
- Total Carbohydrate: 11.4 g
- Protein: 2.5 g

Easy Roasted Cauliflower

"Even my kids will eat cauliflower when I make it like this. Roasting cauliflower in the oven makes it crunchy and the mixture of salt, brown sugar, and curry powder adds a slightly sweet flavor."

Serving: 4 | Prep: 10 m | Cook: 35 m | Ready in: 45 m

Ingredients
- 3 tablespoons olive oil, divided
- 1 head cauliflower, broken into florets
- 1 1/2 teaspoons brown sugar
- 1 teaspoon salt
- 1/2 teaspoon mild curry powder

Direction
- Preheat the oven to 400 degrees F (200 degrees C). Grease a baking sheet with 1 tablespoon olive oil.
- Combine cauliflower and 2 tablespoons olive oil in a bowl. Mix brown sugar, salt, and curry powder in a small bowl. Taste and adjust until mixture is sweet and salty. Sprinkle over cauliflower and mix well. Spread cauliflower in a single layer on the baking sheet.
- Roast in the preheated oven for 20 minutes. Turn cauliflower and roast for an additional 15 to 20 minutes.

Nutrition Information
- Calories: 133 calories
- Total Fat: 10.3 g
- Cholesterol: 0 mg
- Sodium: 625 mg
- Total Carbohydrate: 9.5 g
- Protein: 2.9 g

Easy Savoy Cabbage

"I love savoy cabbage and we serve it as a side to almost anything. This is one of my favorite ways to make it, quick and easy with a little butter and cream."

Serving: 4 | Prep: 10 m | Cook: 10 m | Ready in: 20 m

Ingredients

- 1 head savoy cabbage, sliced
- 3 tablespoons butter
- 1/4 cup heavy whipping cream, or to taste
- salt and freshly ground black pepper to taste
- 1/8 teaspoon ground nutmeg, or to taste

Direction

- Place savoy cabbage in a pot, cover with cold water, and bring to a boil. Cook for 1 minute, remove from heat, and drain. Rinse under cold water. Squeeze savoy cabbage as dry as possible with your hands.
- Melt butter in a pot and add savoy cabbage. Add cream and season with salt, pepper, and nutmeg. Cook until cabbage is soft and creamy, 2 to 4 minutes.

Nutrition Information

- Calories: 189 calories
- Total Fat: 14.4 g
- Cholesterol: 43 mg
- Sodium: 169 mg
- Total Carbohydrate: 14.2 g
- Protein: 4.9 g

Easy Sour Cream Scalloped Potatoes

"Delicious creamy scalloped potatoes that you can make with ingredients around the kitchen."

Serving: 12 | Prep: 10 m | Cook: 45 m | Ready in: 55 m

Ingredients
- 12 large potatoes, peeled and halved
- 2 (10.5 ounce) cans cream of chicken soup
- 2 cups sour cream
- 2 cups shredded Cheddar cheese, divided
- salt and ground black pepper to taste

Direction
- Preheat oven to 350 degrees F (175 degrees C).
- Place potatoes into a large pot and cover with salted water; bring to a boil. Reduce heat to medium-low and simmer until tender, about 15 minutes. Drain. Cut potatoes into cubes and place into a large bowl.
- Stir chicken soup, sour cream, and half the Cheddar cheese into potatoes until evenly incorporated; season with salt and black pepper. Spread potato mixture into a 9x13-inch casserole dish; sprinkle with remaining Cheddar cheese.
- Bake in the preheated oven until cooked through and Cheddar cheese is melted, about 30 minutes.

Nutrition Information
- Calories: 487 calories
- Total Fat: 17.5 g
- Cholesterol: 41 mg
- Sodium: 485 mg
- Total Carbohydrate: 69.9 g
- Protein: 14.5 g

Easy Southern Sweet Potato Casserole

"This recipe is at least as easy as pie, probably easier. Sweet potatoes and sweet marshmallows make for a sweet dish."

Serving: 8 | Prep: 10 m | Cook: 35 m | Ready in: 45 m

Ingredients

- 1 pound sweet potatoes, peeled and cubed
- 1 cup brown sugar
- 1 (10.5 ounce) package marshmallows

Direction

- Preheat oven to 375 degrees F (190 degrees C). Grease a 9x13-inch casserole dish.
- Toss sweet potatoes with brown sugar in a bowl until coated; arrange in the prepared casserole dish. Top sweet potatoes with marshmallows.
- Bake in the preheated oven until sweet potatoes are tender and marshmallows are browned, 35 minutes.

Nutrition Information

- Calories: 270 calories
- Total Fat: 0.1 g
- Cholesterol: 0 mg
- Sodium: 68 mg
- Total Carbohydrate: 68.3 g
- Protein: 1.6 g

Emmas Humongous Yorkshire Puddings

"Being a Yorkshire lass, I take great pride in making these puddings the bigger the better! The only drawback is not having a big enough plate for them!"

Serving: 6 | Prep: 15 m | Cook: 20 m | Ready in: 45 m

Ingredients

- 4 eggs
- 3/4 cup 1% milk
- salt and ground black pepper to taste
- 1 cup all-purpose flour
- 2 tablespoons all-purpose flour
- 2 tablespoons lard

Direction

- Preheat oven to 400 degrees F (200 degrees C).
- Place a muffin tin in the preheated oven.
- Whisk eggs, milk, salt, and pepper together in a bowl. Gradually whisk 1 cup plus 2 tablespoons flour, a small amount at a time, into egg mixture until batter is smooth. Let rest 10 to 15 minutes.
- Carefully remove muffin tin from oven and add lard to 6 muffin cups, about 1 teaspoon per muffin cup. Return to the oven.
- Whisk batter again until small bubbles form on the surface. Carefully remove muffin tin from oven and ladle batter into greased muffin cups, filling almost to the top.
- Bake in the preheated oven until puddings are risen and golden brown, about 20 minutes.

Nutrition Information

- Calories: 185 calories
- Total Fat: 8.1 g
- Cholesterol: 129 mg
- Sodium: 89 mg
- Total Carbohydrate: 19.7 g
- Protein: 7.7 g

Escalloped Pineapple

"My family loves this with pork roast. This dish goes well with chicken or pork."

Serving: 6 | Prep: 10 m | Cook: 30 m | Ready in: 40 m

Ingredients
- 2 cups bread crumbs
- 1 (15 ounce) can pineapple chunks, drained
- 1 cup white sugar
- 1/2 cup margarine, melted
- 2 eggs, beaten

Direction
- Preheat oven to 350 degrees F (175 degrees C). Grease a 1 1/2-quart baking dish.
- Stir bread crumbs, pineapple, sugar, margarine, and eggs together in a bowl. Pour mixture into prepared baking dish.
- Bake in the preheated oven until hot and bubbling, about 30 minutes.

Nutrition Information
- Calories: 471 calories
- Total Fat: 18.6 g
- Cholesterol: 62 mg
- Sodium: 463 mg
- Total Carbohydrate: 70.7 g
- Protein: 7.4 g

Falafelcrusted Cauliflower

"Falafel mix adds earthy depth to roasted cauliflower."

Serving: 3 | Prep: 10 m | Cook: 20 m | Ready in: 30 m

Ingredients

- 1 head cauliflower, cut into florets
- 2 tablespoons olive oil
- salt and ground black pepper to taste
- 1/4 cup dry falafel mix

Direction

- Preheat oven to 425 degrees F (220 degrees C). Line a rimmed baking sheet with aluminum foil.
- Place cauliflower onto the prepared baking sheet. Drizzle with oil, salt, and pepper; toss until coated. Sprinkle on falafel mix; toss until combined. Spread out evenly on the baking sheet.
- Bake in the preheated oven, tossing once, until browned and cooked through, 20 to 25 minutes.

Nutrition Information
- Calories: 162 calories
- Total Fat: 9.5 g
- Cholesterol: 0 mg
- Sodium: 296 mg
- Total Carbohydrate: 16.2 g
- Protein: 7.1 g

Fresh Cranberry Sauce

"A great side dish for Thanksgiving dinner. It can be used as filling for cranberry/cream cheese tarts and also makes a great topping on bagels, corn bread, or cheesecake. Pour into a serving dish or jars and cover. The pectin in the cranberries will make the cranberry sauce gel as it cools. I usually use a fork to mix it up which will make it more pliable."

Serving: 16 | Prep: 5 m | Cook: 15 m | Ready in: 20 m

Ingredients
- 1 cup water
- 1 cup white sugar
- 1 (12 ounce) package fresh cranberries (such as Ocean Spray®)

Direction
- Bring water to a boil in a saucepan; add sugar and cook until sugar is dissolved, about 5 minutes. Mix cranberries into the sugar water; bring to a boil, reduce heat to low, and simmer until desired consistency is reached, about 10 minutes.

Nutrition Information
- Calories: 58 calories
- Total Fat: 0 g
- Cholesterol: 0 mg
- Sodium: < 1 mg
- Total Carbohydrate: 15.1 g
- Protein: 0.1 g

Fried Brussels Sprouts

"Like fried cabbage? Then you are in for a treat. This is easy and most kids are actually surprised that it tastes better than it looks! I add about 2 tablespoons sugar simply to soften the taste and make my kids happy. But it is delicious without the sugar, and when I leave it out, I don't tell them and they never say a word!"

Serving: 4 | Prep: 15 m | Cook: 20 m | Ready in: 35 m

Ingredients
- 6 slices bacon, cut into bite-size pieces
- 1/2 onion, diced
- 1 (12 ounce) package fresh Brussels sprouts, trimmed and sliced
- 2 tablespoons white sugar, or to taste (optional)
- salt and ground black pepper to taste

Direction
- Place bacon pieces in a large skillet and cook over medium-high heat, turning occasionally, until evenly browned, about 10 minutes. Drain on paper towels, leaving grease in the skillet.
- Cook onion in the bacon grease in the skillet until translucent, about 5 minutes. Add Brussels sprouts and toss to coat in the bacon grease. Cook and stir until browned and tender, about 5 minutes. Stir in sugar, salt, and black pepper; sprinkle in bacon pieces.

Nutrition Information
- Calories: 146 calories
- Total Fat: 6 g
- Cholesterol: 15 mg

- Sodium: 379 mg
- Total Carbohydrate: 16.7 g
- Protein: 8.3 g

Fried Buttered Noodles

"This is comfort food at its finest! Serve with roast beef or meat of your choice."

Serving: 8 | Prep: 5 m | Cook: 40 m | Ready in: 45 m

Ingredients
- 1 (16 ounce) package egg noodles
- 1/2 cup butter
- 1/2 cup bread crumbs, or to taste
- salt to taste

Direction
- Bring a large pot of lightly salted water to a boil. Cook egg noodles at a boil until tender yet firm to the bite, about 8 minutes; drain.
- Melt butter in a skillet or large pot over low heat. Add bread crumbs and stir until coated in butter. Mix noodles into bread crumbs mixture. Cook, stirring occasionally, until a crust forms on the bottom, about 30 minutes; season with salt.

Nutrition Information
- Calories: 343 calories
- Total Fat: 14.4 g
- Cholesterol: 78 mg
- Sodium: 162 mg
- Total Carbohydrate: 44.8 g
- Protein: 9 g

Fried Cabbage

"This is a great way to get your family to eat veggies. My son dislikes boiled cabbage, but agrees this is a tasty dish."

Serving: 8 | Prep: 15 m | Cook: 30 m | Ready in: 45 m

Ingredients
- 1 pound bacon, diced
- 2 onions, chopped
- 1 cup diced bell pepper
- 1 head cabbage, chopped

Direction
- Cook and stir bacon, onions, and bell pepper together in a skillet over medium heat until bacon is just starting to brown, about 10 minutes. Add cabbage and cook, stirring frequently, until cabbage is tender and transparent, 20 to 30 minutes.

Nutrition Information
- Calories: 164 calories
- Total Fat: 8 g
- Cholesterol: 20 mg
- Sodium: 460 mg
- Total Carbohydrate: 15 g
- Protein: 9.6 g

Fried Kimchi

"Kimchi is a popular Korean side dish featuring fermented cabbage. Other vegetables can be used and applied with the same fermentation process to produce a similar taste and different textures. In this recipe, I fry some kimchi to completely alter the taste and texture for a smoky doppelganger! It is so great with Korean barbeque and with plain old rice. It is certainly one of my favorites and so easy to make. Enjoy hot or cold! Sprinkle sesame seeds on top as a garnish."

Serving: 4 | Prep: 5 m | Cook: 15 m | Ready in: 20 m
Ingredients
- 1 cup kimchi, chopped into bite-sized pieces, or to taste
- 1/2 teaspoon sesame oil, or to taste
- 1 1/2 teaspoons white vinegar
- 1 tablespoon white sugar, or to taste

Direction
- Heat a nonstick skillet to medium-high heat. Add kimchi. Saute until fragrant and slightly yellow, about 5 minutes. Add sesame oil; cook until kimchi is coated, 2 to 3 minutes. Pour in vinegar to coat the bottom of the skillet. Increase heat slightly; bring vinegar to a boil. Add sugar. Reduce heat to low; cook until sugar dissolves and kimchi is browned, about 3 minutes.

Nutrition Information
- Calories: 25 calories
- Total Fat: 0.7 g
- Cholesterol: 0 mg
- Sodium: 249 mg
- Total Carbohydrate: 4.7 g
- Protein: 0.6 g

Fried Yellow Squash

"Here's a fast and simple way to use up your summer squash (also called crooked neck squash). I have also used this recipe for okra and zucchini. My kids gobble up their veggies this way!"

Serving: 4 | Prep: 10 m | Cook: 15 m | Ready in: 25 m

Ingredients

- 3/4 cup self-rising cornbread mix (such as Martha White®)
- salt and ground black pepper to taste
- 2 yellow squash, cut into 1/8-inch slices
- 1/4 cup olive oil, or more as needed

Direction

- Place cornbread mix in a gallon-size resealable bag; season with salt and black pepper. Add squash, seal bag, and shake to coat evenly. Remove squash from bag and shake off any excess cornmeal.
- Heat about 1/4 inch of olive oil in a large skillet over medium heat. Fry squash in the hot oil, working in batches, until center is cooked and edges are crisp, 2 to 3 minutes per side. Remove with a slotted spoon and drain on a paper towel-lined plate.

Nutrition Information

- Calories: 130 calories
- Total Fat: 4 g
- Cholesterol: < 1 mg
- Sodium: 419 mg
- Total Carbohydrate: 21.2 g
- Protein: 3 g

Frugal Fried Green Tomatoes

"Cheapest way to make fried green tomatoes that are crunchy on the outside, and taste like apple pie on the inside. Great side-dish for any meal!"

Serving: 3 | Prep: 20 m | Cook: 20 m | Ready in: 40 m

Ingredients

- 2 tablespoons vegetable oil
- 1/2 cup cornmeal, or as needed
- 6 green tomatoes, cored and cut into 1/16-inch slices
- salt and ground black pepper to taste

Direction

- Heat vegetable oil in a skillet over medium heat.
- Place cornmeal in a bowl; dip and coat each tomato slice until thoroughly coated.
- Place coated tomato slices side by side in the hot oil; fry until coating is browned and crusty, 1 to 2 minutes per side. Remove with a slotted spoon and transfer to a paper towel-lined plate to drain. Season with salt and black pepper. Repeat with remaining tomato slices.

Nutrition Information

- Calories: 222 calories
- Total Fat: 10 g
- Cholesterol: 0 mg
- Sodium: 34 mg
- Total Carbohydrate: 30.8 g
- Protein: 4.6 g

Garlic Butter Acorn Squash

"This is a savory version of the classic fall flavor of acorn squash!"

Serving: 4 | Prep: 5 m | Cook: 50 m | Ready in: 1 h

Ingredients

- cooking spray
- 2 acorn squash, halved and seeded
- 1/4 cup butter, divided
- 4 teaspoons minced garlic, divided
- salt and ground black pepper to taste

Direction

- Preheat oven to 400 degrees F (200 degrees C). Spray a 9x13-inch baking dish with cooking spray.
- Place each squash half in the baking dish, cut side down.
- Bake squash in the preheated oven for 30 minutes. Flip squash over and place 1 tablespoon butter and 1 teaspoon garlic into each squash. Season with salt and pepper.
- Bake squash, cut-side up until tender, about 20 more minutes. Cool for about 5 minutes before serving.

Nutrition Information

- Calories: 206 calories
- Total Fat: 11.8 g
- Cholesterol: 31 mg
- Sodium: 90 mg
- Total Carbohydrate: 27 g
- Protein: 2.3 g

Garlic Roasted Broccoli

"Flavorful and tasty alternative to broccoli and cheese."

Serving: 4 | Prep: 10 m | Cook: 20 m | Ready in: 30 m

Ingredients

- 1 large head broccoli, cut into florets

- 2 cloves garlic, sliced
- 1 tablespoon extra-virgin olive oil
- 1 pinch onion powder, or to taste
- salt and ground black pepper to taste

Direction
- Preheat oven to 400 degrees F (200 degrees C).
- Toss broccoli and garlic together in a large bowl. Drizzle olive oil over the broccoli; toss to coat. Spread broccoli and garlic onto a baking sheet; season with onion powder, salt, and black pepper.
- Roast in preheated oven for 10 minutes, turn, and continue roasting until beginning to char, about 10 minutes more.

Nutrition Information
- Calories: 62 calories
- Total Fat: 3.7 g
- Cholesterol: 0 mg
- Sodium: 28 mg
- Total Carbohydrate: 6.3 g
- Protein: 2.5 g

German Kohlrabi In Cream Sauce

"This is a classic and easy German kohlrabi recipe that our whole family loves. We eat it as a side to pretty much any meat or fish dish."

Serving: 2 | Prep: 5 m | Cook: 15 m | Ready in: 25 m
Ingredients
- 2 kohlrabi, peeled and thinly sliced
- 1 pinch salt

- 1/2 teaspoon white sugar
- 1/4 cup heavy whipping cream, or more to taste

Direction
- Combine kohlrabi, salt, and sugar in a pot. Set aside until kohlrabi releases liquid, about 5 minutes.
- Cover pot and bring to a boil over medium heat. Shake pot from time to time, so nothing sticks to the bottom. Cook for about 4 minutes. Stir in cream and simmer another 30 seconds without allowing cream to boil.

Nutrition Information
- Calories: 161 calories
- Total Fat: 11.2 g
- Cholesterol: 41 mg
- Sodium: 129 mg
- Total Carbohydrate: 14.3 g
- Protein: 4 g

Gingered Swiss Chard

"I usually don't add much to Swiss chard, as I love its natural flavor, but the addition of ginger brings it up a couple more notches. Hope you enjoy it too."

Serving: 4 | Prep: 10 m | Cook: 11 m | Ready in: 21 m

Ingredients
- 1 large bunch Swiss chard
- 2 tablespoons vegetable oil
- 1 tablespoon freshly grated ginger with juices
- salt to taste

Direction
- Place chard on a flat work surface. Remove large stems and cut into 1/2-inch slices. Chop leaves coarsely.

- Heat oil in a saucepan over medium heat. Add ginger; cook and stir until fragrant, about 1 minute. Add chard stems; cook until tender, about 5 minutes. Toss in chard leaves and season with salt; cook and stir until chard is wilted and liquid is mostly reduced, about 5 minutes.

Nutrition Information
- Calories: 74 calories
- Total Fat: 7 g
- Cholesterol: 0 mg
- Sodium: 185 mg
- Total Carbohydrate: 2.8 g
- Protein: 1.3 g

Glazed Rutabagas

"This is an excellent recipe for an often overlooked and unpopular root vegetable. Even folks who dislike Rutabagas love this delicious dish. Added bonus is this is a great way to introduce this vegetable to kids. A Southern staple with a sweet Asian twist!"

Serving: 3 | Prep: 5 m | Cook: 50 m | Ready in: 55 m
Ingredients
- 1/4 cup butter
- 6 tablespoons brown sugar, or to taste
- 1 cup hot water
- 6 tablespoons soy sauce
- 1 large rutabaga, peeled and cubed

Direction
- Melt butter in a large skillet over low heat; add brown sugar and cook and stir until brown sugar has dissolved.

Stir water and soy sauce into butter mixture, increase heat to medium-high, and bring mixture to a boil. Stir in chopped rutabaga and return to boil.

- Reduce heat to low and simmer, uncovered, stirring frequently, until liquid is absorbed, about 45 minutes.

Nutrition Information
- Calories: 348 calories
- Total Fat: 15.9 g
- Cholesterol: 41 mg
- Sodium: 1974 mg
- Total Carbohydrate: 50 g
- Protein: 5.3 g

Gourmet Wasabi Grits

"My budding gourmet chef husband invented this one morning as a perfect side to his wonderful Lump Crab Meat Swiss Cheese Omelets! Can't wait to serve it to dinner guests with a nice piece of Marinated Steel Head Salmon and steamed Asparagus!"

Serving: 1 | Prep: 5 m | Ready in: 5 m
Ingredients

- 1 (1 ounce) packet instant grits (such as Quaker®)
- 1/2 cup boiling water
- 1 teaspoon wasabi sauce (such as S B® Wasabi)
- salt and ground black pepper to taste

Direction
- Mix grits and boiling water together in a bowl; stir in wasabi sauce, salt, and pepper.

Nutrition Information

- Calories: 119 calories
- Total Fat: 0.3 g
- Cholesterol: 0 mg
- Sodium: 264 mg
- Total Carbohydrate: 25.3 g
- Protein: 2.5 g

Gramas Peppery Parsnips

"This one is for people who like parsnips, and even those who think they don't."

Serving: 4 | Prep: 10 m | Cook: 30 m | Ready in: 40 m

Ingredients

- 1 pound parsnips, peeled, cut in half crosswise, and cut into narrow strips lengthwise
- 1 tablespoon butter
- 1 pinch salt
- ground black pepper to taste

Direction

- Place the parsnips into a saucepan, and cover with water. Bring to a boil, turn down the heat, and simmer until parsnips are tender, 15 to 20 minutes. Drain well, pat the parsnip pieces dry with paper towels, and set aside.
- Melt butter in a skillet over medium heat, and place the parsnips into the hot butter in an even layer. Sprinkle with salt and black pepper (I use quite a bit). Cook parsnips until lightly golden brown on both sides, 5 to 8 minutes per side.

Nutrition Information

- Calories: 111 calories
- Total Fat: 3.2 g

- Cholesterol: 8 mg
- Sodium: 32 mg
- Total Carbohydrate: 20.6 g
- Protein: 1.4 g

Grandmas Armenian Rice Pilaf

"This recipe is my grandmother's. She came from Armenia and it has been in our family for years. We all still make it and it is so easy."

Serving: 4 | Prep: 5 m | Cook: 28 m | Ready in: 43 m

Ingredients
- 1 1/2 cups long-grain white rice
- 3 1/2 cups chicken broth
- 1/4 cup butter
- 1/2 cup crushed Italian vermicelli (very thin noodles)
- salt and ground black pepper to taste

Direction
- Soak rice in a bowl of water for 10 minutes. Drain.
- Bring chicken broth to a boil in a large saucepan.
- Melt butter in a skillet over medium heat. Add vermicelli; cook and stir until brown, 2 to 3 minutes. Add rice; cook and stir until combined, about 1 minute. Pour into boiling broth. Reduce heat to low and simmer, covered, until rice is tender, about 20 minutes.
- Season rice with salt and pepper; fluff with a fork.

Nutrition Information
- Calories: 415 calories
- Total Fat: 12.7 g
- Cholesterol: 35 mg

- Sodium: 965 mg
- Total Carbohydrate: 65.9 g
- Protein: 7.7 g

Grilled Beets With Feta

"Easy way to grill beets!"

Serving: 2 | Prep: 15 m | Cook: 35 m | Ready in: 50 m

Ingredients
- 1 bunch beets, trimmed and thinly sliced
- 1 tablespoon olive oil, or as needed
- 1 pinch sea salt to taste
- 2 ounces crumbled feta cheese
- 2 teaspoons chopped fresh chives, or to taste (optional)

Direction
- Preheat an outdoor grill for medium heat and lightly oil the grate.
- Spread beets onto a sheet of aluminum foil. Drizzle olive oil over beets and season with salt. Fold foil over beets, sealing the edges together to create a packet.
- Cook on the preheated grill, turning once, until beets are tender, about 30 minutes. Carefully open packet and top beets with feta cheese and chives. Close packet again and grill until cheese melts, about 5 minutes.

Nutrition Information
- Calories: 223 calories
- Total Fat: 13.1 g
- Cholesterol: 25 mg
- Sodium: 636 mg
- Total Carbohydrate: 20.8 g
- Protein: 7.4 g

Grilled Broccolimy Kids Beg For Broccoli

"We stumbled on this by accident, and even my kids' friends who 'hate broccoli' love it!"

Serving: 6 | Prep: 10 m | Cook: 5 m | Ready in: 8 h 15 m

Ingredients

- 2 heads broccoli, cut into large florets
- 1 (16 fl oz) bottle balsamic vinaigrette salad dressing (such as Kraft®)

Direction

- Place broccoli and salad dressing in a large resealable plastic bag, squeeze out excess air, and seal the bag. Marinate in the refrigerator for 8 hours, turning bag occasionally.
- Preheat an outdoor grill for high heat and lightly oil the grate. Drain broccoli.
- Grill broccoli on preheated grill until vegetables are tender and browned, turning occasionally, 5 to 7 minutes.

Nutrition Information

- Calories: 274 calories
- Total Fat: 24.4 g
- Cholesterol: 0 mg
- Sodium: 966 mg
- Total Carbohydrate: 14.6 g
- Protein: 2.8 g

Grilled Butternut Squash

"Delicious! Grilling it in slices creates a crispy shell and seals in all the flavor. You don't even need butter or salt and pepper--great on its own."

Serving: 5 | Prep: 10 m | Cook: 15 m | Ready in: 25 m
Ingredients
- 1 butternut squash, sliced into rounds and seeded
- 1 teaspoon olive oil

Direction
- Preheat grill for medium heat and lightly oil the grate.
- Brush both sides butternut squash with olive oil.
- Cook on the pre-heated grill, flipping as needed, until softened and browned, 15 to 20 minutes.

Nutrition Information
- Calories: 100 calories
- Total Fat: 1.2 g
- Cholesterol: 0 mg
- Sodium: 8 mg
- Total Carbohydrate: 23.9 g
- Protein: 2 g

Grilled Butternut Squash With Sage

"This is the best way to have this squash. If you slice it thin and small, it is like chips and smells great. Thicker slices are good for topping with other things at a meal. The grilled squash can also be cut and added to soups for a nice smoked favor."

Serving: 8 | Prep: 10 m | Cook: 8 m | Ready in: 18 m

Ingredients

- 1/4 cup olive oil
- 8 leaves sage, finely chopped
- 1 butternut squash - peeled, seeded, and thinly sliced
- coarse ground sea salt to taste

Direction

- Preheat grill for medium heat and lightly oil the grate.
- Warm olive oil and sage in a saucepan over medium-low heat until sage flavor is infused, 2 to 3 minutes. Remove from heat.
- Brush 1 side of squash slices with sage-infused olive oil. Place oil-side down onto the preheated grill. Brush slices with additional oil. Grill until tender, 3 to 5 minutes per side. Sprinkle with salt.

Nutrition Information

- Calories: 118 calories
- Total Fat: 6.9 g
- Cholesterol: 0 mg
- Sodium: 25 mg
- Total Carbohydrate: 15 g
- Protein: 1.3 g

Grilled Cabbage With Bacon

"A great recipe to take to a potluck. You will need copies of the recipe. Great to set on table for presentation, then cut up so easy to handle."

Serving: 8 | Prep: 15 m | Cook: 35 m | Ready in: 50 m

Ingredients

- 1 head cabbage
- 2 tablespoons butter, or as needed
- 1 sweet onion (such as Vidalia®), chopped
- 1/2 pound bacon, or more to taste
- 1 cup barbeque sauce
- 2 slices bacon, or as desired

Direction

- Cut the knot from the bottom of the cabbage and remove the core.
- Heat 1 tablespoon butter in a skillet over medium heat; cook and stir onion until softened, about 10 minutes.
- Place bacon in a large skillet and cook over medium-high heat, turning occasionally, until evenly browned, about 10 minutes. Drain bacon slices on paper towels, reserving bacon drippings. Chop bacon into small pieces. Mix onion, bacon, and barbeque sauce together in a bowl.
- Fill the hole in the cabbage with onion-bacon mixture and place pieces of butter into the core to fill completely. Drape 2 bacon strips over filling and hold in place with toothpicks.
- Preheat an outdoor grill for medium heat and lightly oil the grate. Make a ring out of aluminum foil and place on grill.
- Place cabbage on the foil ring and cook, basting with bacon drippings, until a fork can easily puncture the cabbage, 15 to 30 minutes.

Nutrition Information

- Calories: 199 calories
- Total Fat: 10.2 g
- Cholesterol: 23 mg
- Sodium: 669 mg
- Total Carbohydrate: 21.8 g

- Protein: 6.4 g

Grilled Cinnamon Toast

"Cinnamon toast with a unique twist. While grilling, the butter mixture caramelizes, and as it cools, it develops a bit of a crunch."

Serving: 8 | Prep: 5 m | Cook: 2 m | Ready in: 7 m

Ingredients
- 1 tablespoon brown sugar
- 1 teaspoon ground cinnamon
- 1/4 cup butter, softened
- 1 (1 pound) loaf brioche
- nonstick cooking spray

Direction
- Mix brown sugar and cinnamon into the softened butter. Spread cinnamon butter over each slice of brioche.
- Preheat an outdoor grill for medium-high heat. Spray grates with nonstick spray.
- Place each slice of brioche on the grill, buttered-side down. Grill until caramelized, 1 to 2 minutes. Transfer to a serving platter.

Nutrition Information
- Calories: 255 calories
- Total Fat: 13.4 g
- Cholesterol: 68 mg
- Sodium: 272 mg
- Total Carbohydrate: 28.2 g
- Protein: 5.6 g

Grilled Foilwrapped Potatoes

"These are a summertime family favorite and are so easy to cook! Great dish that doesn't warm up the kitchen, though you could also make them in the oven."

Serving: 4 | Prep: 15 m | Cook: 10 m | Ready in: 25 m

Ingredients
- 8 slices bacon, cut in half
- 2 potatoes, cubed
- 2 tablespoons butter
- 2 teaspoons seasoned salt

Direction
- Preheat grill for medium heat and lightly oil the grate.
- Place 4 large sheets aluminum foil on a flat work surface. Place 4 pieces bacon in the middle of each sheet of aluminum foil; pile 1/4 of the potatoes on top. Drizzle 1 1/2 teaspoon butter and 1/2 teaspoon seasoned salt over potatoes. Wrap aluminum foil around potatoes to create a pouch.
- Place aluminum foil pouches on the preheated grill; cook until potatoes are tender and bacon is crispy, 10 to 15 minutes. Open pouches carefully.

Nutrition Information
- Calories: 234 calories
- Total Fat: 13.5 g
- Cholesterol: 35 mg
- Sodium: 928 mg
- Total Carbohydrate: 19.4 g
- Protein: 9 g

Grilled Parmesan Asparagus

"Delicious crispy asparagus grilled on an open flame releases the flavor and makes kids love their veggies! You can add or reduce cook time to your liking. Less time will make the asparagus snap more easily, but cooking longer will make them extra crispy and delicious for dipping. Use 1/2 cup melted butter for dipping."

Serving: 4 | Prep: 10 m | Cook: 20 m | Ready in: 30 m

Ingredients

- 1 pound fresh asparagus, trimmed
- 3 tablespoons olive oil
- 1/2 cup grated Parmesan cheese, or to taste
- salt to taste

Direction

- Preheat an outdoor grill on medium heat, and lightly oil the grate.
- Toss asparagus and olive oil in a bowl until evenly coated.
- Sprinkle Parmesan cheese and salt onto asparagus until evenly distributed.
- Place asparagus spears on grill crosswise. Cook until tips are almost blackened, 20 minutes; turning spears over after 10 minutes.

Nutrition Information

- Calories: 157 calories
- Total Fat: 13.1 g
- Cholesterol: 9 mg
- Sodium: 155 mg
- Total Carbohydrate: 4.8 g
- Protein: 6.3 g

Grilled Romaine

"Simple, delicious and is excellent when paired with grilled steak!"

Serving: 2 | Prep: 5 m | Cook: 5 m | Ready in: 10 m

Ingredients
- 1 tablespoon olive oil
- 1 head romaine lettuce, cut in half lengthwise
- 1 tablespoon steak seasoning
- 1 lemon, juiced

Direction
- Preheat grill for medium heat and lightly oil the grate. Drizzle olive oil over romaine lettuce and season with steak seasoning.
- Place lettuce cut side-down on preheated grill. Cook until lettuce is slightly wilted and charred, about 5 minutes. Drizzle with lemon juice to serve.

Nutrition Information
- Calories: 101 calories
- Total Fat: 7.4 g
- Cholesterol: 0 mg
- Sodium: 1390 mg
- Total Carbohydrate: 9 g
- Protein: 2.3 g

Grilled Salt And Pepper Bread

"This is the perfect summertime bread. The grill gives it such delish flavor. We make this to accompany steaks as well as grilled chicken and salads. It's super tasty and very easy. I have to make 2 loaves because it's a favorite. I have toyed with the recipe and added all kinds of spice, but found that good old salt and pepper has the best flavor; go figure! Don't worry about excess butter coating the bread; when the hot loaf comes off the grill, the butter will melt in. We only eat wheat bread, but white would taste just fine."

Serving: 10 | Prep: 5 m | Cook: 9 m | Ready in: 14 m

Ingredients

- 1 loaf French bread
- 1/4 cup butter, room temperature
- salt and ground black pepper to taste

Direction

- Preheat grill to medium.
- Slice loaf lengthwise without cutting completely through the bread. Spread half of the butter on inside surfaces; season with salt and pepper. Coat the outside of the bread with remaining butter; season with salt and pepper.
- Place loaf cut-side down on the grill; toast until browned, checking often, 3 to 5 minutes. Close loaf using tongs. Grill surface until crispy, checking often, 3 to 5 minutes per side.
- Transfer loaf to a cutting board using tongs; slice into 10 diagonal slices.

Nutrition Information

- Calories: 172 calories
- Total Fat: 5.4 g
- Cholesterol: 12 mg
- Sodium: 343 mg

- Heat pot over medium-high heat until milk begins to bubble, then reduce heat to medium-low. Simmer until potatoes are tender, about 20 minutes.

Nutrition Information
- Calories: 332 calories
- Total Fat: 14.4 g
- Cholesterol: 27 mg
- Sodium: 1875 mg
- Total Carbohydrate: 41.4 g
- Protein: 10.7 g

Homemade Dumplings

"Dumplings for stew."

Serving: 6 | Prep: 10 m | Ready in: 10 m

Ingredients
- 2 cups all-purpose flour
- 2 teaspoons baking powder
- 1 teaspoon salt
- 1 cup milk

Direction
- Whisk flour, baking powder, and salt together in a bowl. Slowly pour milk into flour mixture, stirring constantly until dough is stiff and holds together.

Nutrition Information
- Calories: 173 calories
- Total Fat: 1.2 g
- Cholesterol: 3 mg
- Sodium: 568 mg
- Total Carbohydrate: 34.1 g
- Protein: 5.6 g

Honey Dijon Brussels Sprouts

"My mother made this for Thanksgiving. It's a wonderful twist on Brussels sprouts!"

Serving: 2 | Prep: 5 m | Cook: 10 m | Ready in: 15 m

Ingredients

- 10 Brussels sprouts, halved
- 1 1/2 teaspoons butter, melted
- 1 1/2 teaspoons honey
- 1/2 teaspoon Dijon mustard
- 1 pinch dried dill weed
- 1 pinch onion powder

Direction

- Place Brussels sprouts into a saucepan filled with lightly salted water.
- Boil over medium high heat until Brussels sprouts are just tender, 8 to 10 minutes; drain.
- Mix butter, honey, Dijon mustard, dill weed, and onion powder in a large bowl.
- Toss Brussels sprouts in mustard mixture to coat.

Nutrition Information

- Calories: 89 calories
- Total Fat: 3.4 g
- Cholesterol: 8 mg
- Sodium: 78 mg
- Total Carbohydrate: 14.1 g
- Protein: 3.4 g

Honey Ginger Green Beans

"Fresh green beans flavored with honey, soy sauce, garlic, and ginger."

Serving: 8 | Prep: 10 m | Cook: 15 m | Ready in: 25 m

Ingredients

- 2 pounds fresh green beans, trimmed
- 3/4 cup reduced-sodium soy sauce
- 1 tablespoon minced garlic
- 1 teaspoon minced fresh ginger root
- 1 cup honey

Direction

- Bring a large pot of water to a boil; add green beans and cook until bright green and just tender, about 5 minutes. Drain and rinse with cold water.
- Heat soy sauce in a large skillet over medium heat. Cook and stir garlic and ginger in soy sauce until fragrant; stir in honey. Add green beans and toss to coat. Reduce heat to medium-low and simmer until beans are tender, about 5 minutes more.

Nutrition Information

- Calories: 178 calories
- Total Fat: 0.2 g
- Cholesterol: 0 mg
- Sodium: 806 mg
- Total Carbohydrate: 45.4 g
- Protein: 3.5 g

Honey Roasted Carrots With Cumin

"Carrots are tossed with olive oil, cumin, and honey in this simple, easy, and yummy side dish."

Serving: 4 | Prep: 10 m | Cook: 30 m | Ready in: 40 m

Ingredients

- 1 (8 ounce) package baby carrots
- 1/4 cup honey
- 2 tablespoons olive oil
- 1/2 teaspoon ground cumin
- salt and ground black pepper to taste

Direction

- Preheat oven to 425 degrees F (220 degrees C).
- Put carrots into a large sealable plastic bag; add honey, olive oil, cumin, salt and black pepper. Seal the bag and manipulate the contents until the carrots are completely coated; pour into a baking dish.
- Roast in the preheated oven until just tender, or to your desired degree of doneness, 30 to 40 minutes.

Nutrition Information

- Calories: 145 calories
- Total Fat: 6.9 g
- Cholesterol: 0 mg
- Sodium: 84 mg
- Total Carbohydrate: 22.2 g
- Protein: 0.5 g

Honey Roasted Sweet Potatoes

"Sweet and tasty side to any meal!"

Serving: 4 | Prep: 15 m | Cook: 25 m | Ready in: 40 m

Ingredients

- 2 large sweet potatoes, peeled and cubed

- 1/2 cup honey
- 1/4 cup olive oil
- 2 tablespoons ground cinnamon
- 1 tablespoon honey, or to taste

Direction
- Preheat oven to 375 degrees F (190 degrees C).
- Toss sweet potatoes, 1/2 cup honey, and olive oil together in a bowl until potatoes are completely coated. Spread potatoes out on a baking sheet and drizzle any remaining olive oil mixture over the top.
- Bake in the preheated oven until tender, 25 to 30 minutes. Cool on the baking sheet, 5 to 10 minutes; dust potatoes with cinnamon. Transfer sweet potatoes to plates and drizzle with remaining honey.

Nutrition Information
- Calories: 468 calories
- Total Fat: 13.7 g
- Cholesterol: 0 mg
- Sodium: 127 mg
- Total Carbohydrate: 87.7 g
- Protein: 3.8 g

Honey Soy Sweet Potatoes

"A slightly sweet but delicious (and healthy) side dish of sweet potatoes. Especially good with pork."

Serving: 4 | Prep: 10 m | Cook: 15 m | Ready in: 25 m
Ingredients
- 1 large sweet potato, cut into 1/3-inch wide wedges
- 2 tablespoons sesame oil
- 1 tablespoon soy sauce

- 1 tablespoon mirin (Japanese sweet rice wine)
- 1 1/2 teaspoons honey

Direction
- Rinse sweet potato wedges with salted water to soften slightly.
- Heat sesame oil in a large skillet over medium heat. Add sweet potato wedges; cook until light brown, about 2 minutes per side. Reduce heat to low and cover; cook, stirring occasionally, until browned, about 10 minutes.
- Mix soy sauce, mirin, and honey together in a small bowl. Pour into skillet and stir until wedges are evenly coated, about 1 minute.

Nutrition Information
- Calories: 177 calories
- Total Fat: 6.9 g
- Cholesterol: 0 mg
- Sodium: 288 mg
- Total Carbohydrate: 26.6 g
- Protein: 2.1 g

Honey Vanilla Grilled Sweet Potatoes

"A great way to bring a normally fall side right into spring and summer. The flavors are light and simply delish!"

Serving: 4 | Prep: 10 m | Cook: 25 m | Ready in: 35 m

Ingredients
- 2 large sweet potatoes, peeled and thinly sliced
- 3 tablespoons butter, melted
- 2 tablespoons ground cinnamon
- 1/3 cup honey
- 1 tablespoon vanilla extract

Direction

- Preheat grill for medium heat.
- Arrange sweet potatoes in a 9x13-inch aluminum foil pan. Stir butter and cinnamon together in a bowl and drizzle over potatoes. Cover pan with aluminum foil.
- Bake sweet potatoes on the preheated grill, stirring occasionally, for 15 minutes. Stir honey and vanilla extract together in a bowl and drizzle over sweet potatoes. Return aluminum foil to cover pan. Continue cooking on the grill until sweet potatoes are tender, about 10 more minutes.

Nutrition Information

- Calories: 375 calories
- Total Fat: 8.8 g
- Cholesterol: 23 mg
- Sodium: 188 mg
- Total Carbohydrate: 72.1 g
- Protein: 3.9 g

How To Make Farinata

"Farinata is nothing more than a simple garbanzo bean flour batter which is spiked with olive oil and salt and baked in a very hot oven. The surface gets crusty, the edges get crispy, and yet the inside stays moist and sort of creamy. The texture is easy to explain, but the taste, not so much. Very earthy, comforting, and satisfying."

Serving: 6 | Prep: 10 m | Cook: 25 m | Ready in: 35 m

Ingredients

- 1 1/2 cups garbanzo flour
- 2 cups lukewarm water

- 1 1/2 teaspoons kosher salt
- 1/2 teaspoon minced fresh rosemary (optional)
- 5 tablespoons olive oil, divided
- freshly ground black pepper to taste

Direction

- Combine garbanzo flour and water in a bowl; whisk until batter is smooth. Cover bowl with plastic wrap or a plate and let stand at room temperature for 2 hours. Skim as much foam as possible from top of batter. Whisk salt, rosemary, and 3 tablespoons olive oil into batter.
- Preheat oven to 500 degrees F (260 degrees C).
- Place a 10-inch cast-iron skillet over high heat and heat until smoking hot. Pour 2 tablespoons olive oil in skillet and swirl to coat bottom of skillet with oil. Continue to heat until oil shimmers and a wisp of smoke rises from oil.
- Quickly pour batter into hot oil; carefully transfer skillet to preheated oven.
- Bake in the preheated oven until cake is browned and crusty, 25 to 30 minutes. Transfer immediately to a plate, cut into wedges, and serve hot. Garnish with freshly ground black pepper.

Nutrition Information

- Calories: 190 calories
- Total Fat: 12.3 g
- Cholesterol: 0 mg
- Sodium: 483 mg
- Total Carbohydrate: 15.1 g
- Protein: 5 g

Instant Pot Corn On The Cob

"This method probably isn't any faster than the traditional method of boiling corn, but I can put everything in the pot

Instant Pot Mashed Potatoes

"Make the best mashed potatoes you've ever tasted with this quick and easy recipe. The cream cheese makes them extra velvety, a trick I picked up from my brother Mike."

Serving: 6 | Prep: 10 m | Cook: 20 m | Ready in: 40 m
Ingredients

- 6 russet potatoes, peeled and cut into chunks
- 1/4 cup cream cheese
- 1 tablespoon cream cheese
- 1/4 cup milk
- salt and ground black pepper to taste

Direction
- Place a steamer inside a multi-functional pressure cooker (such as Instant Pot(R)). Add 1 cup water to the pot. Place potato chunks into the steamer. Close and lock the lid. Select Rice function and set timer for 10 minutes. Allow 10 to 15 minutes for pressure to build.
- Release pressure using the natural-release method according to manufacturer's instructions, 10 to 40 minutes. Unlock and remove lid. Add 1/4 cup plus 1 tablespoon cream cheese and milk to the pot and mash using an electric hand mixer or a potato masher. Season with salt and pepper.

Nutrition Information
- Calories: 271 calories
- Total Fat: 4.6 g
- Cholesterol: 14 mg
- Sodium: 80 mg
- Total Carbohydrate: 52 g

- Protein: 7.3 g

Jacobs Roasted Broccoli

"Roasted broccoli topped with lemon juice is a quick and easy side dish that only requires 5 ingredients and is a simple addition to any meal. This recipe was made in a Panasonic CIO and appears on an episode of the Dinner Spinner TV Show on The CW!"

Serving: 4 | Prep: 10 m | Cook: 8 m | Ready in: 18 m
Ingredients
- 1/4 cup olive oil
- 1 teaspoon salt
- 1/2 teaspoon ground black pepper
- 2 heads broccoli
- 4 teaspoons fresh lemon juice

Direction
- Preheat oven to 425 degrees F (220 degrees C).
- Whisk olive oil, salt, and pepper together in a bowl.
- Separate broccoli florets from stem. Trim and discard bottom off stem. Peel stem with a vegetable peeler or paring knife and slice cross-wise into 1/4-inch-thick pieces. Add florets and stems to oil mixture and toss to coat. Arrange broccoli mixture in a single layer on a baking sheet.
- Roast in the preheated oven until tender, 8 to 10 minutes. Sprinkle lemon juice over roasted broccoli.

Nutrition Information
- Calories: 172 calories
- Total Fat: 14.1 g

- Cholesterol: 0 mg
- Sodium: 631 mg
- Total Carbohydrate: 10.6 g
- Protein: 4.3 g

Jalapeno Creamed Corn

"Corn with a zip!"

Serving: 6 | Prep: 5 m | Cook: 10 m | Ready in: 15 m

Ingredients
- 1/2 (8 ounce) package cream cheese
- 1/4 cup butter
- 2 (11 ounce) cans whole kernel corn
- 1 cup shredded Cheddar cheese
- 1/4 cup diced jalapeno chile pepper

Direction
- Melt cream cheese and butter together in a saucepan over medium heat; add corn, Cheddar cheese, butter, and jalapeno pepper. Cook the corn mixture, stirring regularly, until the sauce is smooth and the ingredients are hot, about 10 minutes.

Nutrition Information
- Calories: 293 calories
- Total Fat: 21.4 g
- Cholesterol: 61 mg
- Sodium: 479 mg
- Total Carbohydrate: 20.3 g
- Protein: 8.9 g

Jicama Zebra Fries

"Ever wonder what to do when you have too much jicama? Here's a quick guide to making a quick snack. Best served with barbeque sauce. The stripes on the fries are caused by the moisture escaping the jicama and creating fissures where the starch from the jicama collects and browns."

Serving: 2 | Prep: 10 m | Cook: 10 m | Ready in: 20 m

Ingredients

- cooking spray
- 1 cup French fry-sized pieces of jicama

Direction

- Spray a microwave-safe plate with cooking spray. Arrange jicama pieces on plate.
- Cook in the microwave on high until small brown stripes begin to form on the fries, 9 to 11 minutes. Check on the fries every few minutes to avoid burning. Remove plate from microwave with an oven mitt because plate will be hot.

Nutrition Information

- Calories: 26 calories
- Total Fat: 0.2 g
- Cholesterol: 0 mg
- Sodium: 3 mg
- Total Carbohydrate: 5.7 g
- Protein: 0.5 g

Josephs Best Easy Bacon Recipe

"Preparing this recipe is literally the first thing I do after I wake up on weekend mornings. I put the bacon in the oven (must be cold!), brush my teeth, start cooking other breakfast items, and then take the bacon out after 14 minutes - that's it! My bacon theory is that by placing the bacon in a cold oven to start, as the oven gradually heats to 425 degrees F (220 degrees C), the bacon undergoes a magical transformation from cold flabby piece of meat, to simmering deliciousness, to crispy bacon heaven as the oven hits the 425 degree mark. Enjoy!"

Serving: 6 | Prep: 5 m | Cook: 15 m | Ready in: 25 m

Ingredients

- 1 (16 ounce) package thick-cut bacon

Direction

- Line a large baking sheet with 2 sheets of aluminum foil, making sure pan is completely covered.
- Arrange bacon strips on the prepared baking sheet, keeping at least 1/2-inch space between strips. Place pan in the cold oven.
- Heat oven to 425 degrees F (220 degrees C). Cook bacon for 14 minutes.
- Transfer cooked bacon to paper towel-lined plates. Let cool for 5 minutes for bacon to crisp.

Nutrition Information

- Calories: 134 calories
- Total Fat: 10.4 g
- Cholesterol: 27 mg
- Sodium: 574 mg
- Total Carbohydrate: 0.4 g
- Protein: 9.2 g

Kingombo Patatas

"This dish originated in Africa but my mother and her relatives prepared it in Alabama. Kingombo is the name of okra in the African Bantu language and patata is the name of potato in Spain. I combined the two words together to name my dish. This is a wonderful okra and potato dish that can used as a side dish or it can be eaten for breakfast. Enjoy kingombo patatas!"

Serving: 8 | Prep: 15 m | Cook: 10 m | Ready in: 25 m

Ingredients
- 1/2 cup cornmeal
- salt and ground black pepper to taste
- 2 large potatoes, cut into 1/2-inch cubes
- 1 pound fresh okra, trimmed and cut into 1/2-inch pieces
- 1 white onion, finely chopped
- 1/2 cup cooking oil

Direction
- Mix cornmeal, salt, and pepper together in a large resealable plastic bag; add potatoes, okra, and onion. Seal bag and shake until vegetables are coated with cornmeal mixture.
- Heat cooking oil in a large skillet over medium heat until shimmering but not smoking. Place vegetables in the hot oil and cook until potatoes are tender and okra and onion are browned, 10 to 12 minutes. Transfer cooked vegetables to a paper towel-lined plate using a slotted spoon.

Nutrition Information
- Calories: 133 calories

- Total Fat: 1.7 g
- Cholesterol: 0 mg
- Sodium: 30 mg
- Total Carbohydrate: 26.9 g
- Protein: 3.6 g

Lazy Green Peas

"My wife introduced me to microwaved frozen peas. Life hasn't been better since."

Serving: 2 | Prep: 5 m | Cook: 3 m | Ready in: 8 m

Ingredients

- 1 cup frozen peas
- 1 tablespoon shredded Italian cheese blend (such as Wegmans®)
- 1 teaspoon nutritional yeast, or more to taste
- 1 pinch garlic powder, or to taste
- salt and ground black pepper to taste

Direction

- Heat frozen peas in a small microwave-safe bowl on high in the microwave until hot, about 3 minutes.
- Stir Italian cheese blend, nutritional yeast, and garlic powder into peas; season with salt and black pepper.

Nutrition Information

- Calories: 77 calories
- Total Fat: 1.3 g
- Cholesterol: 3 mg
- Sodium: 193 mg
- Total Carbohydrate: 11.3 g
- Protein: 5.5 g

Lemon Honey Glazed Carrots

"Baby carrots cooked in a honey, butter, ginger, and lemon glaze. This goes really well with peppercorn steak and cheesecake."

Serving: 4 | Prep: 5 m | Cook: 20 m | Ready in: 25 m

Ingredients

- 1 pound baby carrots
- water to cover
- 1/4 cup butter
- 2 1/2 tablespoons honey
- 1 tablespoon lemon juice
- 1/8 teaspoon ground ginger

Direction

- Bring carrots and enough water to cover to a boil in a saucepan; reduce heat to medium-high and continue to simmer until carrots are tender, about 10 minutes. Drain and set aside.
- Melt butter in a large skillet over low heat; stir in honey. Add lemon juice and ginger. Increase heat to medium and stir in carrots until well coated. Continue cooking until thickened, about 5 minutes more.

Nutrition Information

- Calories: 182 calories
- Total Fat: 11.7 g
- Cholesterol: 31 mg
- Sodium: 170 mg
- Total Carbohydrate: 20.4 g
- Protein: 0.9 g

Lemonglazed Carrots

"Very easy and quick to make!"

Serving: 2 | Prep: 10 m | Cook: 10 m | Ready in: 20 m

Ingredients

- 2 carrots, sliced 1/4-inch thick
- 1 tablespoon butter
- 1 tablespoon brown sugar
- 1 teaspoon lemon juice
- salt and ground black pepper to taste (optional)

Direction

- Place carrots into a large pot and cover with water; bring to a boil. Reduce heat to medium-low and simmer until carrots are tender, about 8 minutes. Drain.
- Heat butter in a skillet over medium heat; cook and stir carrots, brown sugar, and lemon juice in the melted butter, stirring often, until sugar has dissolved, 2 minutes.

Nutrition Information

- Calories: 102 calories
- Total Fat: 5.9 g
- Cholesterol: 15 mg
- Sodium: 85 mg
- Total Carbohydrate: 12.7 g
- Protein: 0.6 g

Printed in the USA
CPSIA information can be obtained
at www.ICGtesting.com
LVHW010822190224
772167LV00002B/326